4/23/04

Stanley Frank

Frankly Speaking

Stanley Frank:
Greensboro's Quiet Benefactor

Ned Cline

Stanley and Dorothy Frank Family Foundation
Greensboro, N.C.

To Dorothy,

a most unselfish person,
a devoted and loving wife
and mother who continues to excel
in bringing happiness
to family and friends

Table of Contents

1

Bumpy Start, Smooth Finish

Stanley Frank learned early that life does not provide a free ride.

As early as his teenage years, he was taught to work hard, show responsibility and earn his own way if he expected to succeed. Nobody was going to hand him a ticket to anywhere. For him, those lessons were well learned and have never been forgotten.

Frank's father, Hugo, walked away from the family when his son Stanley was an infant, barely three months old. The departure came amid unsubstantiated rumors of infidelity involving Hugo Frank and a friend of his wife's family. While never supported with facts, those rumors forced the father out, ended the marriage and left an unresolved bitterness that lasted until the parents' deaths. From the day his father left until the day he died 48 years later, Stanley Frank's mother and father never saw or spoke to each other again.

As a new single parent, Adele Loeb Frank first

worked as a seamstress. She was forced to leave her children with relatives because her job required spending a week at a time, sometimes more, in the homes of customers for whom she made clothes for entire families. She later completed a hair styling school course and became a beautician, a profession that brought in a few more dollars and allowed her to remain at home each night with her son Stanley and his older sister Betty.

In the first years after her marriage failed, Adele Frank and her children lived with her sister's family as one way of saving money while she worked as a seamstress. They continued that living arrangement for five more years while she rented space for her beauty shop before being able afford to move into her own apartment with the beauty shop in the front and living quarters in the rear.

The mother's meager income, plus $6 a week in child support payments from their absentee father, was the family's sole source of income during Frank's formative years.

Although Frank's single mother struggled financially, she never gave up or sought sympathy. Rather, she gutted it out with determination and a strict set of disciplinary rules. Those were traits her son remembered on the road to his own professional and personal successes.

"I never really felt deprived when I was growing up because I always had enough food and clothes and I didn't need much else," Frank said of his early years. "I never felt any great need beyond the basics, but I did have to learn the importance of pinching pennies. Those experiences, though, taught me significant lessons about honesty, dedication to goals and

values, and the importance of solid family relationships."

As a high school student, Frank earned his first
income —25 cents a week — by stopping by the post
office in the community of Tottenville, New York, each
afternoon on his way from school to pick up the mail
for a neighbor, Mrs. Hillard. "I did that every school
day for two years," Frank said. "That was the only way
I was able to have any money for myself, a dollar a
month. The post office was more than a mile from
Mrs. Hillard's home and she paid me a quarter a week
so she wouldn't have to bother going to get her mail
on cold, rainy days."

Frank's first job as a high school graduate in
July 1931 paid him $15 a week, part of which he gave
his mother for household expenses. The company that
employed him was caught in the financial struggle of
the early years of the Great Depression; Frank accepted
two pay cuts, down to $12.82 a week, before the com-
pany finally went bankrupt and closed in January
1933.

His next job paid even less, $10 a week, 25 cents
an hour for a 40-hour week as required by the gov-
ernment-inspired National Recovery Administration.
His first car was a used, well-worn 1928 Studebaker
that he bought for $20 from a jobless family man who
needed the cash for food for his children a lot more
than he needed transportation.

From that fitful, yet important, no-excuses-al-
lowed start, Frank learned the value of diligence, determination and dedication toward achievement. Also
from that beginning he realized the importance of finding financial success for his own family and later leaving a positive, lasting impact on his community.

Stanley Frank traveled that long and sometimes difficult financial road from his early years on Staten Island by way of Richmond, Virginia, to his adopted hometown of Greensboro, North Carolina, in 1936. Once he came South, he took an essentially bankrupt, non-mainstream business, Carolina By-Products Company, which transformed inedible animal by-products into usable and useful consumer goods, and turned it into a profitable enterprise that set new, higher standards for that industry nationwide. He became one of central North Carolina's most respected as well as energetic corporate executives, albeit much less well known than some others who sought public recognition.

He also showed by example that positive leadership could serve useful roles on worthy community endeavors ranging from managing an airport, helping with the formation of a professional sports team, and assisting with the strengthening of three college campuses, all adding value to the lives of those around him.

There is little debate among business and civic leaders in Piedmont North Carolina about who deserves a large share of the credit for development of and progress at the user-friendly commercial passenger and freight airport, Piedmont Triad International, located between Greensboro and Winston-Salem. People familiar with the airport's growth are effusive in their praise of Frank's long and dedicated work at that facility and give him most of the accolades for its success. He modestly demurs, saying he was just one of many people responsible.

Among the half dozen most significant donors to Guilford College, Frank and his wife, Dorothy, are near the top of the list. He is among the strongest boosters of Wake Forest University and the University of North Carolina at Greensboro in terms of financial contributions and hours devoted to campus projects. Support for and allegiance to those schools help balance the missing ingredient, a college degree that Frank was never able to afford as a young man.

As he built his business and served as a community volunteer and leader, he also built a reputation for honesty, integrity and seemingly unbounded energy. Past his middle 80s at the beginning of the 21st century, Frank was still serving on dozens of boards and commissions and dispensing advice on multiple projects throughout Piedmont North Carolina. During the last half of the 1900s, when there was a community project which needed to be done in or around Greensboro, Frank was more often than not one of the first to step forward. Seldom did he ever just say no when asked to help.

He has for decades served as a mentor for those who sought to follow his lead. "I've done what I always thought was the right thing, even if it was not always popular at the time," Frank said of his philosophy and his approach to business and community projects. "I know I've made mistakes. But I hope that what I have been able to do has helped my community become a better place for more people."

Those who have followed his career say Frank undervalues his contributions. Modesty, though, has been one of his enduring traits. Most of what he has accomplished through a long series of civic and philanthropic endeavors has been done without an abundance of public recognition. Most of his contributions have not been headline producers, mostly by design.

As Frank and his wife entered their twilight years at the end of the 20th century, they reflected on what they had achieved and looked at ways to continue their contributions for future generations. In early 1998, they created a private family foundation, under the umbrella of the Community Foundation of Greater Greensboro, in order to preserve their sizable assets for the benefit of people and organizations that will remain after Frank, his wife and two childless sons are gone. The foundation began providing needed community resources shortly after its creation and modest contributions were continuing through the early years of the 21st century. But the largest donations, by design, will come after the family is deceased.

"My family and I have all we need and want," Frank said of his motivation in creating the philanthropic foundation. "I don't believe in spending money needlessly on myself or my family. I learned that early in life. We don't lack for anything essential. As the saying goes, a man can't eat but one steak a day. I see no advantage in having to run to the coast or mountains to a second home. I've got a nice home right here. I've been fortunate and able to make a good living with Greensboro as home for our company, which, when I owned and operated it, grew nationally and internationally. I'd rather leave our family assets for the benefit of this community whose people have helped me become successful. I think it's important to give something back as a way of showing appreciation for the good fortune we have had."

The Frank Family Foundation will be the vehicle to accomplish that goal.

2

Early Years

Three weeks to the day after Stanley Frank's birth in New York, on a continent half a world away, two pistol shots rang out, signaling the start of World War I. It was the summer of 1914.

Three years later, with bloody battles still raging and a once-reluctant United States military fully engaged in the trench fighting, toddler Frank stood on the sidewalks of the Bronx and watched gun-carrying *doughboys,* as the American soldiers were called, marching to build support for the war effort.

"That's the first memory I have," Frank said. "I remember the soldiers marching, in formation. I didn't know what it meant then, but I later learned the troops were marching to raise the spirits of the American people. Our country felt a strong need to continue the fighting. Those soldiers must have made quite an impression on me, for I recall them so vividly. My mother told me this parade of young men was important even though I was too young to understand the significance at the time."

The American war effort succeeded, on the battlefield and in the hearts of supporters back home. Frank's Jewish relatives were abundant in their dedication to America's war sacrifices because so many of the family members had experienced first-hand the humiliations of class and economic discrimination in their native Germany.

Frank's mother, Adele Loeb, was one of five daughters of German Jews who came as young adults to America in the first decade of the 20th century. The family lived in the small town of Griesheim, in western Germany, along the Rhine Valley near Darmstadt, south of Frankfurt. However, they all left home in search of a better economic and social life; they also escaped from what they feared as the pending persecution of Jews in Germany. They came with limited financial resources, but armed with hope and manual skills learned as teenagers in German trade schools.

The sisters arrived in New York at different times. Bertha, the oldest, came first. Adele was the second to arrive. The other three — Selma, Paula and Rachael — arrived in America between 1900 and 1910. Two other siblings, a brother and sister, had died as children before the turn of the century. Two other brothers, who chose not to join their siblings in the United States, later fled to South America from Germany, when Hitler came to power prior to World War II and began his infliction of hatred and death on Jews.

The Loeb daughters left their parents, Maier and Betty Strauss Loeb, behind in Germany, and came to America with the parents' reluctant blessings and words of caution and advice on how to live in their new land. Their father sent his daughters a letter, in

German script, with his advice on how they should conduct themselves in this country. That letter, kept within the family for more than 50 years, has since been lost.

Frank's maternal grandmother, Betty Strauss Loeb, was a descendent of one of the musical Strauss family brothers. She could not recall in later life which brother so Frank family members have never known that exact family linkage.

All five sisters who came to America showed ambition and determination. When they arrived in New York, none could speak a word of English; they each learned the language in night school to replace their native German. Four of the five married in the United States; one never married.

Two of the sisters were dressmakers, one was a milliner, and a fourth worked for a company listed on the New York Cocoa and Sugar Exchange. The fifth married shortly after coming to this country and became a fulltime mother.

Affluent, society-connected families in New York favored in-home seamstresses and Adele Loeb's skills with a needle and thread helped her reputation spread as a superb dressmaker. For years she was in demand as a seamstress who lived in the homes of her customers as she stitched clothes for women and girls — hard work for not much money.

Stanley Milton Frank was born June 7, 1914, in New York City. The big news of that day in and around Manhattan was a sailboat race among some of the city's richest residents, with Cornelius Vanderbilt and J.P. Morgan among the losers. In North Carolina on that date, the top news story was the state Democratic Party's adoption of a strongly worded anti-progressive, conservative political platform that would have made later Republicans proud.

Frank's birth was a mere 21 days before the war was started with the bullets in Bosnia. His country and his family would be caught up in the war effort during the years of his early life. His parents, German Jews, had come to this country a decade ahead of the war in an effort to escape the escalating religious and economic discontent among warring factions in their native land. The Franks understood the importance of personal freedom in the United States, freedom that had been denied them in Germany.

Frank's father and uncles didn't join the United States World War I effort as soldiers because age and marriage responsibilities made them ineligible. But their patriotism and allegiance to the American war efforts in support of European Allies was pronounced.

"They were all very pro-America after coming to this country and adopting it as their new land," Frank said of his family members. "They strongly supported American involvement in the war." (Later, a subsequent war, World War II, would come closer to the family's heart because of Hitler's reign of terror against Jews and, more personally, because a nephew, a navigator and bombardier, was shot down while flying combat missions over Europe.)

In 1918, as the wounds of World War I began to heal, Frank's financially strapped single mother moved with her two young children from the Bronx into her sister's home in Tottenville, a small family-oriented neighborhood on the southern edge of Staten Island. That would be their home for another decade. It was their second such move out of economic necessity by the time Stanley was four and his sister Betty was seven.

The two moves were brought on because of a shortage of financial resources with a wage-earning father no longer part of the family. Frank's mother could not afford rent for an apartment, so she moved herself and her two children into the cramped living quarters of relatives in the Bronx. Still unable to support her children four years later when the relatives moved to Tottenville, the Franks made the move with them.

Frank isn't clear on the exact circumstances of his father's departure; he was too young at the time to know, and his mother steadfastly throughout her life refused to discuss even sketchy details with him. "It wasn't something we mentioned in our home," Frank said. "All I know is that they were divorced, and the one condition for granting divorce in New York in those days was adultery."

Hugo Frank never visited the residence of his wife and children once he left in the late summer of 1914. "My mother didn't hate people, but she sure had some very strong feelings about my father," Frank said. "It was not pleasant. My parents never saw or spoke to each other after my father left. There was never any personal contact." Hugo Frank did, however, routinely mail his former wife a weekly child support check for $6.

Frank later said he had learned enough about his father from other family members to believe that some inappropriate conduct caused the marriage breakup. But he has never been convinced his dad was guilty of all the actions alleged by his mother's family. "He was really not a bad person," Frank said, "but he did like a good time. Although it may be extreme to call him a playboy, I think he did have a habit of chasing women. He didn't drink alcohol. His eye for women was probably his worst bad habit."

There was ample speculation within the family at the time that Frank's father was, in fact, falsely accused by a jealous brother-in-law who may have had his own desires for the woman that Hugo was accused of successfully wooing and later married. Whether guilty or not, Frank's mother believed the worst of the stories she was told about her husband and ordered him out of the house.

"While my mother never discussed the circumstances with me," Frank said of the breakup of his parents' marriage, "I have always had the feeling that she had been told some things about him that were not all true. She was a very trusting person and she believed what she was told. I won't say my father didn't have a girlfriend while my mother was pregnant with me because I obviously don't know for sure. But I tend to doubt that he would have left my mother on his own volition. In comparing my mother and his second wife, while they were both fine people, I would have to say my mother was certainly the superior person."

When Stanley Frank was 21, he finally met his dad. He and his sister Betty, with an abundance of anxiety about the outcome, made initial contact by letter. The children knew where their father lived because he listed his return address as Washington on the envelope of his child support checks. Those envelopes contained only the support payment, never any letter or other written expression of concern about his children.

After Betty Frank wrote their father, he agreed to meet his children in New Jersey while he was on vacation with his second wife, the woman with whom he was accused of having the illicit affair during his first marriage. Their mother didn't approve of the meeting, but she didn't attempt to prevent it because both children were at the time adults.

Even after the son and father met for the first time more than 20 years after Hugo Frank had left his family, they never established any semblance of a father-son relationship. Later, ironically, they developed a long-lasting business relationship. Once Frank was established in his own business in North Carolina, he learned his dad was out of work in Washington. Frank then hired his father, who worked as a laborer for more than two decades until his retirement and death.

"I never had any feeling or attachment to him as a father," Frank said of his dad. "He was just another person. In fact, I didn't have any particular feeling about him one way or the other. He was friendly, laid back, a good worker, although not especially ambitious. I never had any particular resentment about his leaving our family, although my mother surely did. But I never considered him a father — I never really knew how a boy was to look toward his father since I never had had a father when I was growing up. In later years, he was simply an acquaintance and an employee. But he was never what I would call a father."

When Frank's mother, Adele, a determined woman with strict rules about the importance of running a household, moved her two siblings into the home of her sister's family in Tottenville, she set up a regimented schedule that was both grueling and essential. The transition gave young Stanley and his sister exposure to an extended family and allowed at least some new freedoms.

Their new place of residence in Tottenville was

a step up from the Bronx apartment. This ten-room house was on Arthur Kill Road, a main thoroughfare that ran much of the length of Staten Island. The Franks shared the home with Adele's older sister Bertha, her husband Willie Ascher, and their daughter, Beatrice.

While not especially fancy for that time and place, the home had inside plumbing, a coal-burning stove in the kitchen, central heat, and, near the kitchen stove, a huge wash tub, in which the women scrubbed clothes by hand.

While less than five years of age at the time, Frank recalls another vivid memory that sticks in his mind just as the marching troops did earlier in the Bronx. It is what he still calls "the big explosion."

Just across the river from Staten Island in Morgan, New Jersey, a vicious explosion in the fall of 1918 at a munitions factory sent the entire region into a panic out of fear of other, more damaging, blasts. For safety, Frank and other family members huddled in a small basement room for several days for fear that additional explosions would send fireballs or debris onto nearby rooftops and injure people on the streets or

Simson Frank, Stanley Frank's grandfather, born February 20, 1831, died August 10, 1907, in Germany.

in their homes. There was also fear that an explosion would cause a tall chimney hovering over a Tottenville smelting plant to collapse onto the home where the Franks then lived. The basement was considered the only safe place in their house.

Franks' mother and her sister went upstairs each day just long enough to prepare meals, then returned to the safety of the basement. The munitions explosions continued inter-

Emile Frank, Stanley Frank's grandmother, born March 1, 1847, died October 6, 1911, in Germany.

Hugo Frank, Stanley Frank's father, in the early 1900s.

mittently for three days before normalcy returned to the neighborhood. "Aside from the troops marching, the other thing that has stayed vivid in my memory from my earliest recollections is the fear from those explosions," Frank said.

•

The Frank family story shares much with

21

the story of the Loebs. Within a year or so of the five Loeb sisters coming from Germany to New York, three children of Simson Frank made the journey to America from their native land. Brother Hugo stayed in New York and two sisters, Sara and Mina, settled in Savannah, Georgia. As a teenager, Simson Frank had come from Germany earlier in the 1800s and settled in Texas, where he acquired land holdings. Sketchy oral family history passed down through the generations suggests that Simson Frank was doing quite well financially with his Texas ranch holdings. But success was fleeting.

Sometime in the last quarter of the 19th century, Simson Frank — displaying some of the unsettling traits that his son Hugo would later show — abruptly announced to his ranch employees that he was returning to Germany for what he said would be a short while. Simson later told family members he grew homesick for Germany and wanted to honor his mother's request that he return home.

The Frank family had a long history in that part of Germany, dating back thousands of years to what was known as the "Glockenbecher" culture of 2000 BC. In fact, in 1977, archaeologists digging in a 1,000 year-old graveyard in Griesheim, near Darmstadt, uncovered a well-preserved skeleton from a nomadic culture that roamed Western Europe nearly 4,000 years ago. That skeleton was identified from a grave in what was identified as the Frank section of the cemetery. The Franks, a Germanic tribe, had settled along the lower and middle Rhine, near Darmstadt, as early as the third century. Some of the tribe among Stanley Frank's ancestors remained in Germany while others relocated to what is now France in the late fourth century, giving that country its modern name.

Once Simson Frank returned to his native land,

he never left and died in Germany in 1907 at the age of 73. His land holdings in the United States were ultimately turned over to his hired help. Subsequent generations of Frank family members were told that Simson Frank's Texas land was of significant value when he returned to Germany, but no ownership rights were retained by the family.

"We once checked on what was supposed to be his (Simson's) assets but were told everything was worthless," a cousin wrote in one undated letter to Stanley Frank's sister Betty. That land later proved to be very valuable — under subsequent owners — after oil was discovered.

Simson Frank married Emile Wasserman shortly after returning to Germany, a marriage that produced son Hugo and daughters Sara and Mina. Emilie died in Germany in October 1911, four years after her husband's death, without ever seeing America.

Hugo Frank and his two sisters were all born in Germany within a few years after their father returned from the United States. Despite their father's dislike for America, in 1905 the three Frank teenaged siblings had heard enough from their father to convince themselves they wanted to come to America. So they left their native Battenhausen. (The hometown of Henry Kissinger, President Nixon's Secretary of State and special adviser, Battenhausen is a small city not far from Ulm, Germany.)

•

There was no land and certainly little money when Adele Loeb and Hugo Frank met in New York, introduced by mutual friends, and were married in 1910. Their daughter Betty was born one year later and son Stanley three years after that.

By the end of the war, however, the rumored illicit marital indiscretions of Hugo — real or perceived — had split the family.

With her husband gone, resources limited and the need to leave home for days at a time because of her seamstress job, Adele Frank determined her only option for family stability was to move in with her sister's family. That move would ensure that her young son and daughter could get family care while she was away from home, and she could save rent payments.

Adele's sister Bertha didn't work outside the home and she was able to serve as the surrogate mom to Stanley and Betty while their mother was away making clothes for affluent New York families.

"I can still see (my mother) leaving home, carrying her little sewing kit, to walk about a mile to meet the train, even in the cold and snow. She would be gone for a week at a time," Frank said with sadness in his voice. "It was hard on her. She worked terribly hard to provide for us, even without rent payments. It still hurts me deeply to think of what all she had to do to keep the three of us together."

Frank, however, has never accepted any feeling of pity nor has he allowed the label "poor" to be attached to his family. "We had the basics," he said, "because my mother worked very hard to make that happen. I never realized we were poor. We had plenty to eat and all we really needed. I never thought of us as poor."

Frank had regular chores at his uncle's home in those years, ranging from shoveling coal into the furnace to painting the house. But he also had time for play, after finishing daily homework assignments, and was a member of an organized baseball team in his teens. He was a second baseman; his arm wasn't strong enough for shortstop or third base. He was also what he said could kindly be called a "weak" hitter. A yellowed newspaper clipping among his personal papers shows he once — but only once — got two hits in one game off an opponent's best pitcher.

Frank's toughest financial struggle would actually come later as a young adult with his first fledgling, low-paying jobs as the years of the Great Depression were sucking companies into red ink, and the unemployment lines were growing. For a time, Frank was one of thousands standing in unemployment lines.

The titular head of the Frank household in Stanley's early years was his uncle William Ascher, an accountant for Tottenville Copper Company, a smelting plant in which zinc, copper and lead were melted and turned into telephone cables. The company later became part of the Western Electric Company.

Adele Frank and her two children lived with William and Bertha Ascher for a decade as the mother saved what money she could in hopes of moving out on her own. She did that, but not until 1924 after she was established as a beauty shop owner.

Young Stanley Frank began his school life in Tottenville, first as a five-year-old kindergarten student. He was clearly a bright student and had continuing academic success, despite a strong streak of independence and a bit of devilment. His kindergarten teacher was Miss Page, whom he described as a "tall, skinny thing" who endured private ridicule from her students. Behind her back, Frank was among those who referred to their teacher as "Bitty" Page.

Frank completed all academic requirements for eight years of elementary school six months early and finished four years of high school work in three and one half years, graduating in 1931 at age 17.

Frank credited his early completion of all required classroom assignments to hard work rather than extraordinary talent. But there seems little doubt that he had a knack for certain courses even while he eschewed others not to his liking.

"I mostly took those academic courses that appealed to me," Frank explained, rationalizing his independent actions. "I took Latin for a short while, and one day the teacher said any of us who didn't like the course should just leave. I walked out. I never went back to that Latin class."

Frank once was directed by school officials to take a course in Algebra in high school. "I hated it," he said. "I started a class in Geometry. Hated it, too, so I quit both classes. I took commercial arithmetic and was delighted with it. That's the kind of knowledge I needed throughout my business career. Geometry wouldn't have done me a bit of good."

After walking out on his Latin course, Frank completed the equivalent of four years of German during his three and one half years in high school. That language, compared to Latin, was a snap because his mother and other relatives spoke German at home.

After more than a decade with her sister and brother-in-law, Adele Loeb Frank concluded that handmade dressmaking wasn't as fashionable as it once was and realized her income, never high, was dropping steadily. She decided to take up hair styling. She completed a beauty school course and opened her own hairdressing shop, initially in a storefront on another part of Staten Island, in a community called Great Kills.

Five years after opening her own shop, she finally felt financially able to move her two children out of her sister's home. With a lease on her beauty shop space on Amboy Road in Great Kills, the Frank family moved there. The shop was in the front, with living quarters in the rear of the building. The rave for New York women in those days was a new hairstyle known as the permanent wave. Frank said his mother made more money giving permanent waves than she did making dresses.

The Franks lived in the rear of the beauty shop for about three years before moving to another rental home on Hillside Drive in another section of Great Kills, where they resided when Stanley graduated from high school. That was also where he experienced his first exposure to organized religion, but it wasn't Judaism.

Stanley's closest friend during his final high school years was Fred Schnackenberg, a Lutheran. The Frank rental home was across the street from a Lutheran church. Because his mother wasn't a practicing Jew and didn't observe Jewish beliefs, young Stanley attended Lutheran Sunday school each week with his pal Fred. Synagogues and Jewish holidays were foreign to him.

"Not many Jews lived in our immediate neighborhood when I was growing up and my mother had gotten away from her religion after coming to this country," Frank said. "I went to the Lutheran church and that was fine with me. My mother never objected because my recollection is that there was never any relationship in our family with our Jewish religion. My mother and her sisters never practiced the faith. As a child I was never in a synagogue or temple. I don't recall that anyone in our family ever celebrated any of the high holy days." That would change for him after his marriage.

Before he developed any adherence to the Lutheran faith, however, Frank set his sites on his own employment to help his mother with living expenses; he could not afford college. His friend Schnackenberg enrolled in college fulltime, planning to be a Lutheran minister. The two remained friends for several years, but drifted apart as Frank concentrated on his work and Schackenberg dug into college life. It was more than 25 years later that Frank learned his friend had shifted from ministerial studies to government work and had wound up as an official in the Pentagon.

The Frank family ties to the Lutheran church lasted through several generations. Betty Frank married Walter Uphaus, a Lutheran; she adopted that religion for the remainder of her life even after she and her husband divorced. Betty and Walter, whom she had met in New York, lived in various cities, including Greensboro for several years, while Uphaus worked for Burlington Industries.

That marriage produced one son and daughter. The daughter, Betty Adele, who was named for her mother and grandmother, continued in her mother's faith and married a Lutheran minister, Daniel Lindstrom. The Lindstroms live in Eugene, Oregon. Son Robert Uphaus lives in East Lansing, Michigan, where his mother chose to live following her divorce. Betty Uphaus died in the winter of 1996 in East Lansing.

Frank's earliest jobs in New York were not much to brag about in terms of pay or prestige. His first job didn't last long because the company went bankrupt, partly because of the nation's sluggish economy and partly from what he feels was corruption by some investors.

Those were all early experiences not to be repeated — nor forgotten. They were worthy experiments to be learned from and put to good use in a later and far more profitable time.

3

Digging for Dollars

Earning a high school diploma ahead of schedule was relatively easy for an energetic Stanley Frank, especially after he junked those academic courses he didn't like and concentrated on those in which he excelled.

But that was in 1931, on the heels of the worst economic collapse in the nation's history. Job seekers far outnumbered the available openings, and finding work that would last or provide enough income for even the basics was no easy task.

Searching with little success in the summer of 1931, he sought the help of friends and found work through what would a half-century later become popularly known as networking. Frank, of course, had never heard of that term at the time; he just knew he needed help.

His uncle, William Ascher, with whom he had lived as a youngster, knew someone who was a friend of a man who ran an insurance company. Several conversations and several months later, an anxious yet determined Stanley Frank landed his first job that provided a paycheck, meager though it was, as a junior underwriter for an insurance corporation, Union Indemnity Company.

Union Indemnity was considered at the time to be one of the country's finest, though that perception was false, as young Frank would regrettably learn the hard way.

The company was run by an experienced and respected insurance executive, Luther Van Allen, and had a heavy market in Massachusetts, where collecting premiums was a problem. An affiliated company, New York Indemnity, which dealt primarily in homeowner's coverage, was in the same shape.

While Van Allen was the chief operating officer of the company, a kingfisher political figure from the deep South actually controlled it. That man was Huey Long. As history has repeatedly shown, Long pulled a lot of financial strings in the business and political world, leaving numerous crinkled knots along the way.

During the 1930s, Long, of course, launched several generations of his family's political dominance in Louisiana and Washington. Less than a year after being elected governor of his home state in 1928, Long was impeached by the Louisiana House of Representatives for misuse of state money. But his more favorable political connections with his state's senate resulted in his acquittal on the impeachment charge, and he remained in office and power in his home state before moving on in 1930 to what would eventually become a prominent place in national politics.

Just how Long gained control of Union Indemnity was never made clear to Frank. But what was clear was that the company was in deep financial difficulty despite the fact that Long, using his political clout in Washington, had secured a $32 million government loan from the Reconstruction Finance Corporation, a federal agency, to help keep the company afloat. Congress founded the RFC in 1932 to make loans to businesses as one means of recovery from the Great Depression. Set up to close after ten years, the RFC lasted until the late 1950s and dealt with various allegations of political favoritism during its lifetime. Long was one of the first to get political favors from that agency.

Long got the government cash, but Union Indemnity didn't get much of an extended life. Within the company there was speculation, but no proof, that at least some of the millions in public money never got far from Long's own pockets. On January 6, 1933, 18 months after Frank went to work, Union Indemnity went broke and closed its doors. Employees had one day's notice: they were told at the end of one shift that the office would close at the end of the next day. Less than two years out of high school with no income and no other business experience, Frank found himself walking from one employment line to the next in search of work.

Frank's job as an underwriter during his short tenure before bankruptcy at Union Indemnity was a tedious, tenuous one. He was called a junior underwriter, but he never sold any insurance policies. Instead, he was given a desk and a stack of policy applications. He sat there, day in and day out, adding up figures on a manual calculator, the kind with the single crank handle. His starting pay was $15 a week. That wasn't much but was more than he had ever made before. "And given the circumstances in the country at the time, that wasn't bad pay for a kid just out of high school," Frank later conceded.

In retrospect, from a businessman's seasoned eyes, Frank can point to signs from the beginning of the job that things were not going well for the company. During his 18 months on the job, he was forced to take two pay cuts in order to retain his post. When the company went bankrupt, he was being paid $12.82 cents a week. It took more than three years following the bankruptcy, after Frank had moved south and was living in Greensboro, for his final week's pay from Union Indemnity to arrive, paid by the New York State Insurance Department.

Four decades later, while on a business trip to Manhattan, Frank walked past the former Union Indemnity offices at 100 Maiden Lane. Headquartered in that building were offices of American International Group (AIG), one of the country's best known and strongest insurance conglomerates, which has ties to

Frank's hometown. United Guaranty Corporation in downtown Greensboro, where Frank was an original investor, is a wholly owned subsidiary of AIG.

That trip to New York City brought back memories of his early days, and Frank could only wonder what might have been if the federal government loan to Huey Long had been able to save Union

Stanley Frank, with his sister Betty, at their Staten Island home, late 1919.

Indemnity and he had never come South.

Out of work and broke at age 18, Frank frantically sought ways to earn an income. The prewar decade established clear alternatives for men in Frank's situation. A person worked or went hungry. Individual enterprise was encouraged. That's another lesson Frank has never forgotten.

As desperate as Frank was, others were worse off. At least he had no family to support, as did many other jobless men in New York. That's when he learned of an unemployed father of two daughters who was so much in need of money for food for his children that he was offering a deal to the first buyer: a 1928 two-door Studebaker sedan for $20. That car was the only asset the man had to sell.

Seizing the opportunity, Frank bought that used car, the first one he had ever owned, with the few dollars he had saved added to a few more borrowed from his mother and sister. With his car as his office, Frank became an on-the-road peddler, first of steel wool pads and then of Graphol, an oily liquid poured in gas tanks supposedly to help auto engines last longer.

Commercial laundries had begun using steel wool in cleaning processes in the early 1930s on the theory that the pads would transfer heat from pressing machines to clothes much better than cloth would. That theory didn't prove true, at least for Frank. He was a somewhat less than successful salesman, not from lack of effort but primarily from lack of customers with money to buy his products. After two months on the road, he had completed only one large sale to a restaurant chain that operated its own laundry for table cloths and napkins.

Frank quickly determined that he couldn't make a living pushing steel wool pads, but he had a $20 Studebaker that would run. He turned to a different product, choosing Graphol, a forerunner to the auto engine lubricant STP. Loading up the back seat of his Studebaker sedan with Graphol containers, he traveled the roads of New Jersey, marketing his wares to service stations. Gasoline prices, about 9 cents a gallon, were cheaper in New Jersey than across the river in New York, and Frank found selling easier and less hectic there.

But squeezing out a regular income on the hopes that gas station operators and automobile owners had a few dollars for engine lubricants wasn't especially rewarding, financially or personally. For nine months, Frank rotated between peddling his products and standing in unemployment lines.

"Oh God, it was terrible and humiliating," Frank said, describing his search for regular work. "I would sit there in the employment office, hour after hour and day after day, waiting and hoping that someone would offer me a job."

In August 1933, while waiting in yet another line at a Manhattan employment office, Frank picked up a discarded copy of *The New York Times* and spotted a classified ad from a company looking to hire an office boy. That wasn't much, but it was more than he had.

He rushed from the unemployment line to the desk of his sister, who had a job at Chase Bank, and asked her to type him a letter asking for that job. He mailed the letter and waited three weeks for a reply.

The day before Labor Day, 1933, Frank received a one-cent postcard that said simply: "Report to John

Boyle & Company on Reid Street in two days." Frank showed up early on the designated day, was interviewed by the company president, John Boyle Bell, and told to go home and await an answer.

Two days later, Frank received a second penny postcard offering him a job and asking him to report for work the next day. He later learned he was one of 1,000 applicants for that single job and the only one to receive an offer. He said he was never brave enough to ask if he was hired because he was considered superior to the other applicants or because the company president determined he was more desperate for work than the others. The only thing that mattered was that he had a job.

Frank's starting salary was less than he was making with the insurance company, but it was certainly better than hawking steel wool pads or auto engine lubricants with no guarantee of any income.

His first paycheck from John Boyle & Company as an office boy/errand runner was $10 a week, 25 cents an hour for a 40-hour week, the minimum required by the National Recovery Administration (NRA). The NRA was one of President Franklin Roosevelt's first steps in his New Deal policies aimed at government assistance toward private industry's economic recovery. The agency attempted to enforce codes of fair competition for businesses, beginning in 1933. The U.S. Supreme Court in 1935 ruled the Recovery Administration unconstitutional, and Roosevelt abolished it.

During its short life, however, the NRA helped ensure Frank at least a minimum income and for that he was grateful.

John Boyle & Company, unlike Union Indemnity Insurance, didn't have Huey Long meddling in its financial affairs and was on relatively solid ground for the Depression years. The company made window awning material and marketed it across the country. Among its company plants was one in Statesville, North Carolina.

Stanley Frank, age 7, with his sister Betty, age 10, 1921.

Frank's initial job title of office boy accurately fit his assignments. From his mother's home in the Great Kills neighborhood of Staten Island, he caught the train to the boat landing, then rode the ferry on a 20-minute trip to Manhattan, walked to the post office, picked up the company mail bag, carried it across his shoulder, and walked the half dozen blocks to the company offices — by 8 a.m. On days when he had extra coins, he paid a nickel to ride the trolley from the ferry slip to the post office.

Six months of efficient mailbag duty and punctuality were enough to show company owners young Frank had potential for other responsibilities, and he was asked if he'd like to learn the company's bookkeeping system. He eagerly said yes because it eliminated the post office stop and gave him a few more dollars each week in his paycheck.

The new assignment took him from the mailroom to the accounting department, where he began helping balance company financial ledgers. His performance there was such that he was offered a second promotion, one that gave him exposure to other parts of the company operation. Clearly, company owners felt he was a valuable enough employee that he should learn more about the business.

Frank was sent to the packaging department where purchase orders were assembled and wrapped for shipping. That job taught him to identify parts and distinguish between a 531-awning stripe and a 267 stripe. It was his bosses' way of teaching him the business. Both Frank and his supervisors assumed he would be there a long time.

The new assignment also meant a salary increase to $23 a week, the most money he had ever earned. He called it "big money" for 1934, enough to allow him to pursue a long-sought desire of getting more education. Frank enrolled in night classes at Columbia University. He worked all day and sat through English and economics courses at Columbia three nights a week before returning home to Staten Island.

Frank had been at John Boyle & Company approximately a year when, shortly after he turned 21, his sister took an action that changed his life and his future.

Sister Betty, by then married, spoke for the first time with her brother of her long-held desire to meet their absentee father. Betty suggested they make contact with him by letter, hoping he would respond but unsure if he would. She wanted to see, she said, if their father still cared for them, if he would be willing to meet them. Betty barely remembered their father; she had not seen nor heard from him since she was three years old. Stanley, only an infant when his father left home, didn't remember his father at all, but he agreed that his sister should attempt to make contact, despite the uncertainty of the result.

Their mother opposed the meeting but didn't overrule the letter seeking it, perhaps thinking or more likely hoping such a gathering likely would never occur. Fearful and anxious, Betty Frank Uphaus wrote her letter on June 8, 1934. Her words make clear her desire as well as her concerns.

> *Dear Father:*
>
> *I have been wanting to write to you for several years, but just never got the letter written. As you can readily see, it is very difficult for me to write this letter as I don't remember you but still I feel that I know you very well.*
>
> *Both Stanley and myself are old enough now to realize how unfortunate the entire situation was. I can see into it still better now inasmuch as I am very happily married and my relatives tried very hard to interfere. There is a very long story attached to this and I will not go into detail now. Mother is very happy about my marriage.*
>
> *To come down to the reason for my writing. Stanley and I are very anxious to see you and wonder whether you would like to see us. If you don't expect to come to New York perhaps we can arrange to come to Washington. You need not fear that there is any hidden motive. Our only reason is the fact that we want to know our father. Mother*

has told us much about you.

Hoping to hear from you, I am

Your daughter,

Betty

The response was both prompt and positive. Hugo Frank, then working at an animal fat rendering plant in Washington, D.C., wrote back within days that he'd be pleased to see his children, absent their mother.

A poignant indication of the father's private appreciation for that letter surfaced 60 years later, long after Hugo Frank's death. He had kept — and apparently cherished — that letter the remainder of his life but never had told his family he saved it. In early 2001 Stanley Frank was surprised to find a copy of the letter among his father's personal papers, decades after his father's death.

Frank would later say his father's willingness to meet his children deeply hurt his mother. The father gave them a date when he and his new wife Bertha would be vacationing in Atlantic City, New Jersey, relatively close to their home. Another exchange of letters arranged the date and place to meet: on the Jersey beach, in the late summer of 1934.

That initial father-son meeting was cordial but in no way emotional. It was, Frank later recalled, merely pleasant and friendly, not unlike a first meeting of any two strangers. No personal feelings emerged from either side, just a handshake and general conversation over lunch at the hotel where the couple was staying. "He seemed happy to see me," Frank said

Stanley Frank, age 13, upon his graduation from grammar school, January 1928.

of that meeting. "I was glad to see him. But there was no attachment either way. He was just another person, a stranger."

Neither then nor later did either of the two ever mention the circumstance of the father's leaving his family.

Hugo Frank learned in that initial meeting that his son had a job, making $23 a week at an awning company. The son learned his dad was moderately successfully employed in the animal fat rendering business. The father also may have sensed that his son had ambitions beyond packaging awning material or keeping up with window decoration hardware and financial records.

"When do you get a vacation?" the father asked.

"In August of next year," the son replied.

"Well, how would you like to come down to Washington and spend some time with me, to see the city?" Hugo asked.

"I'd like that," Stanley responded. He, of course, had never seen Washington and was looking forward to seeing the city as much as to spending a week with the stranger who was also his father.

What Stanley Frank didn't know was that his dad had an ulterior motive in asking his son to visit.

Hugo had privately concluded in his initial meeting and conversation with his son that Stanley might be interested in moving to a different part of the country. The trip to Washington was eventful for several reasons. The end result was the fulfillment of both a successful, enduring vocation and avocation, neither a long time coming after that trip.

Stanley Frank had been fascinated with airplanes since his early teen years, but he had never been on one until he visited his dad in August 1935. Even in his late 80s, Frank remembered virtually every detail of his maiden flight more than 65 years earlier.

Frank flew from Newark, New Jersey on a beautiful, sunny Sunday morning to the nation's capital, to what was then called Hoover Airport, located near the center of the city. A city street ran perpendicular to the single runway and when planes landed, a gate similar to a railroad crossing was dropped to halt auto traffic so incoming planes could swoop down safely and land before taxiing across the highway to the terminal. Frank flew on Eastern Air Transport, a forerunner to Eastern Airlines, on a DC 2, 14-passenger plane. The ticket price was $14.

The airfield was later relocated further from the center of the city, across the Virginia line, and renamed Washington National. In the late 1990s the name was changed again to the Reagan National Airport in honor of former President Ronald Reagan.

Frank's flight to Washington would be the first of thousands he would take during his adult life, many in his own plane, and would be the beginning of a long and pleasant love affair with planes and airport economy.

The first stop in Washington was what Frank

described as the "very nice" apartment of his father at 4007 Connecticut Avenue, NW. Before the day was out, the two wound up at Hugo's place of employment, a rendering plant on K Street, not far from affluent Georgetown and the Potomac River, where the senior Frank was plant manager. Stanley Frank had never seen a rendering plant until that day and was not particularly impressed.

Frank, at his father's urging, spent as much of that week talking about converting animal waste products to usable household or farm products as he did touring the city or talking the city's primary industry of politics.

Frank learned that week of his father's work during the two decades since he had been ordered out of the home of his family. First, Hugo had worked as an independent dealer in and grader of cattle hides, having earned a reputation as an expert judge of quality cowhides and calfskin. But independents like him couldn't compete against established dealers in a New York market where large dealers shut out smaller entrepreneurs.

Hugo purchased hides from slaughtered cattle in New York and drove across the river to New Jersey, where the market was more open. Most of his hides were sold to Harry Therbold, who operated an animal waste rendering plant in South Kearney, New Jersey.

Half a century before Hugo Frank started his buying and selling of animal waste products in New Jersey, a man named Louis Hopfenmaier opened a rendering plant in the District of Columbia; this financially successful business was passed to his son Milton. Milton Hopfenmaier had married Hugo Frank's sister, Sara, but had died at a relatively early age in his 40s, leaving a widow with a huge estate and little knowledge of how to manage it.

Sara Hopfenmaier called her brother Hugo for help. "You've got to come down here and help me," she pleaded with her brother. He agreed and ended his cattle hide business in New York and New Jersey to begin helping run a rendering plant not far from the White House.

The business continued to succeed, as did Sara's interest in a future husband, a respected Washington businessman, Herbert Guggenheim, who had intimate social ties with some of the city's most influential leaders and who had been an executor of her husband's estate. Sara Hopfenmaier married Herbert Guggenheim not long after her brother Hugo arrived to help run the business.

The two men worked well together, but it was clear Hugo was in the shadow of his brother-in-law. Hugo had no social connections in the nation's capital and sought none. He remained a loyal plant manager but never attempted to step beyond those bounds.

Herbert Guggenheim, on the other hand, was well known and well liked among the Washington inner circle, despite a personality that some considered the equivalent of coarse sandpaper. He and wife Sara lived in splendor in the Wardman Park Hotel, later the Sheraton Park on Connecticut Avenue, NW.

Guggenheim's unpleasant personality was established among his fretful employees, who frequently felt intimidated by a managerial style that was generally overbearing and unbending. At home with Sara, however, he was meek, mild and humble because his wife demanded it. "Aunt Sara kept him in his place at home," Frank said. "I was always proud of her for that.

He was rough and hard to please at work, but never at home." Frank agrees with those who say Guggenheim privately suffered from an inferiority complex, and was gruff and obstinate to his employees as a way of compensating for his own insecurity.

One of Guggenheim's best friends was Clark Griffith, owner of the Washington Senators. The two had daily poker games. Griffith and Guggenheim were together watching a World Series game in 1953 in Yankee Stadium when Guggenheim suffered a fatal heart attack.

While visiting in Washington in August 1935, Stanley Frank was introduced to Guggenheim, who had been tipped off by Stanley's father that his son wasn't enamored of New York. But the introduction didn't produce immediate rapport. Rather, they were more like sugar and the shark.

"Hey, kid, whatcha doing in New York?" was the rude, initial Guggenheim greeting to his nephew through marriage.

A mild mannered and slightly intimidated young Stanley gave a brief history of his job status, stressing the successes instead of the failures.

Stanley Frank, New York, 1935.

"Your father asked me to ask you about whether you wanted a job down here. Do you?"

"Well, I'm doing okay in New York, but I would consider leaving."

"If you want to come and work for us, we can send you down to Richmond. We can pay you $15 a week, but no more. You interested or not?" Guggenheim didn't waste words.

Frank thought for a moment, but not much longer. The $15 starting salary was disappointing because it would take him back to where he started with the insurance company four years earlier. But he quickly calculated that living costs would be less in the South and he foresaw greater opportunity with the rendering company, despite its unpleasant reality of foul odors and its perceived poor reputation among those outside the industry.

"Okay, I'll take the job," Frank responded on the spot, perhaps surprising even himself with the rapid reply about a new life and lower pay. But he was ready to abandon New York, which had never had any particular appeal to him, and that was incentive enough to accept the new challenge.

Frank knew his decision would not make his mother happy. He would be moving away from her home and closer to his father. She would not approve of either. But he was an adult and she would just have to accept his decision. Frank would later say he never really anticipated any particular relationship with his dad. Time, however, would provide them a chance for contact that neither at the moment realized. The same was later true for Frank and his mom.

Guggenheim's company, Richmond Refining Company, operated a satellite rendering plant in Richmond, Virginia. One of the by-products was laundry soap produced from animal fats. That plant had a contract with the state of Virginia to produce soap for all the state prisons, a guaranteed market that would likely only grow. While Frank knew virtually nothing about the rendering business, he knew that making soap was simple enough by mixing water, caustic soda and grease.

Frank returned to New York, resigned his job in the packing room of John Boyle & Company, and made his way South in September 1935 — to become a laborer at the Richmond rendering plant. For his return and permanent trip South, Frank took the train to Washington. While he would have preferred flying, the train was cheaper than the $14 airfare. That was important because he was, after all, taking a pay cut of $8 a week.

Stanley Frank, age 21, his mother Adele, and sister Betty, New York City, fall 1935, the week Frank left his native New York and moved South to start his new career.

The move to a different part of the country, even with lower pay, was the start of something big. With a certain amount of fear and trepidation sandwiched around his high expectations, Frank was starting a new life that would ultimately be exceedingly rewarding.

4

Hot Grease & Cold Animals

Stanley Frank arrived in Richmond, Virginia, to begin his new career on Sunday, September 29, 1935. His father Hugo drove him from Union Station in Washington to Richmond to meet his new boss, Harry Barker, manager of the rendering plant there.

Barker had a far more pleasant personality than grumpy Uncle Herbert Guggenheim, but later that same day and early the next on the first day on the job Frank began to wonder if he had made the right move.

"I found you a place to stay," Barker told his new employee, driving Frank to the room he was to rent in the home of another Barker employee. To put it mildly, the place was depressing. Frank's room had no heat and the house was dilapidated. Daily breakfasts consisted of what the overweight homeowner referred to as a "poor man's" meal of biscuits, gravy and molasses. The menu never changed.

At work, Frank's first assignment regardless of

the weather was as a grease route helper, operating out of a 4-cylinder International truck with no doors. His job was to visit the rear entrances of restaurants and pick up garbage cans full of grease, most of it left over from baking Virginia hams, and haul it to the rendering plant where it was cooked as part of the soap-making process.

At the end of each day's grease route, Frank had a second duty of sweeping the floors in the soap production room. Lifting vats of grease all day and breathing in soap dust that agitated his nostrils every night was tough enough. His next set of duties was even tougher but all part of his learning process.

After a few months on the grease route, Frank was reassigned to what was called the dead stock room, where dead animals retrieved from farms — horses, cows, mules and hogs — were processed into household products or animal feed ingredients. When animals died at nearby farms, the rendering plant was called to haul them away. Frank was the man handling the pick up duty.

Hides of the dead animals were removed for curing and sale, and body parts were removed for rendering into animal feed and tallow. When there were no dead animals to be removed from farms, Frank spent his hours delivering 100-pound bags of ingredients for poultry and hog feed to farm supply stores in the Richmond area.

Four months to the day after starting his rendering plant job in Richmond, Frank received an unexpected phone call that changed his life again. The call, while he was on a feed ingredient delivery run, reached him at 4 p.m. It was from Harry Barker's office assistant, a tough-talking, no-nonsense Mrs. Eaton, who ordered Frank to report to the company's struggling rendering plant in a town called Greensboro in North Carolina. He was to be there by 8 a.m. the next morning. "I had no advance notice or warning of that move," Frank later explained. "Mrs. Eaton said, 'Get there,' and that was it. Harry Barker was plant manager, but Mrs. Eaton pretty much ran the place. When she said something, we didn't question it. We just did it."

Frank finished his delivery route and returned to the plant where Barker had a train ticket to Greensboro waiting for him. He went to his boarding house room where he changed from his dingy overalls and boots to his one set of dress clothes. He packed his work clothes in a paper bag and within hours climbed aboard the late night train that put him in North Carolina — for the first time — the next morning at 7 a.m.

That was Tuesday, January 28, 1936.

Until he was assigned to Greensboro, Frank was not even aware that the company had a rendering plant in the city. What he would soon learn, however, was that the Greensboro operation was an extremely weak link in the chain of the company's four animal-fat rendering and tallow plants.

Some three decades earlier, E. L. Field had purchased two rendering plants in Virginia, Richmond Refining and Norfolk Tallow. By the late 1920s, because of the Depression, Field had run into financial difficulty and was deeply in debt to the estate of Milton Hopfenmaier in Washington and the rendering plant there managed by Herbert Guggenheim. To cover the Field debt, the Hopfenmaier estate, with Guggenheim in control, assumed 51 percent of the ownership of the two Field Virginia rendering plants.

E.L. Field was later killed in an auto accident and his brother John A. (Jack) Field took over management of the Virginia plants. It was Guggenheim and Jack Field who extended their business southward to Greensboro when they created Carolina By-Products Company.

The Greensboro rendering plant was started at the request of the City of Greensboro, which, like many cities across the country and particularly the South, opened an abattoir during the Depression years of the late 1920s. When the nation's economy turned sour and the private cattle markets all but evaporated, these cities took on such non-profitable projects as a means of helping farmers market their animals.

Once the Greensboro abattoir opened in 1928 on Randolph Avenue, just east of South Elm Street, city officials and the local Chamber of Commerce went industry hunting. They contacted Jack Field in Richmond with a request that he open a rendering plant to process non-edible animal parts and wastes left over from the city's slaughtering operations. The city was interested only in slaughtering animals for farmers and wanted someone else to handle the wastes. Field and Guggenheim agreed to the city's request and, in 1928, opened the Greensboro plant under the name of Carolina By-Products. The beginning was, at best, inauspicious as owners sought to squeeze out slim profits. The business tilted on the verge of financial collapse for years.

Field and Guggenheim, unhappy with the limited revenue after 18 months, wanted out of the Greensboro business in the early 1930s. They signed an agreement to sell the Greensboro operation to Louis Fleischer, a private businessman in Macon, Georgia. Fleischer also struggled for years to make the business go, but he was never able to pay off his debt for the purchase price. Field and Guggenheim were forced to resume ownership in 1935.

The Greensboro rendering plant, small by industry standards at the time, was located at 2410 Randolph Avenue in the southeast quadrant of the city, next door to the city-run abattoir. The city charged farmers a fee for slaughtering animals at the abattoir, gave edible parts to owners and then sold the leftovers to the rendering plant.

Carolina By-Products in the late 1940s purchased the abattoir from the city at the request of city councilman Ben Cone and leased it to Curtis Brothers (later Curtis Packing) Company, operating next door. Both Curtis Packing and Carolina By-Products were still operating on the same sites at the beginning of the 21st century.

When Field and Guggenheim resumed ownership of the Greensboro rendering plant in 1935, they assigned Field's other brother Fred as manager in hopes of turning a profit. That decision only made a bad situation worse.

Fred Field was often missing during working hours and had a poor management habit of firing some of his best workers without cause. Plant profits were dwindling as surely as dead animal parts were recycled. What Jack Field and Herbert Guggenheim would later learn was that Fred Field was an alcoholic who spent as much time tipping booze bottles as he did transforming vats of animal grease into usable consumer products.

That was the precarious situation at Carolina By-Products when a young Stanley Frank was given the few hours' notice to pack his bags and move to

Greensboro to work at the plant.

When Frank arrived at the Greensboro train depot on that frosty January morning in 1936, a reasonably sober Fred Field met him.

"He put me in the car and said we had to go get the truck and begin the route of picking up kitchen grease and other wastes from meat markets," Frank said of his first look at Greensboro. "I told him okay, but that I really needed to change clothes. I was wearing my dress clothes and carrying my work clothes in a bag."

Field drove Frank to the nearby Texaco gas station owned by Joe Melvin, father of future Greensboro mayor Jim Melvin, on Asheboro Street; Frank changed clothes in the men's toilet. Joe Melvin, later tragically shot to death at his station during a robbery, loved to tell people he introduced Frank to his new city by showing him the toilet.

Frank and Field spent their first day together in a run-down Dodge truck, the only vehicle the Greensboro plant owned, picking up grease and inedible animal parts from restaurants and butcher shops in Greensboro, High Point and Winston-Salem. The plant had only two routes, one in and around Greensboro and one in the Chapel Hill-Durham-Raleigh area.

Frank spent his first night in Greensboro in Field's home. The next day he rented a room at Mrs. Leora M. Feree's boarding house at 338 Church Street. The rate was $6 a week, about 40 percent of his weekly salary, but it included a hot breakfast (consisting of something other than biscuits and gravy) and supper every evening. Mrs. Feree's was known as a comfortable place for bachelors in the city, even though Frank parked his animal waste truck behind the house each night. That truck was Frank's only means of motorized transportation during his first months in Greensboro. He couldn't afford his own car.

Guggenheim remained concerned about the Greensboro plant and frequently telephoned Frank at night at Mrs. Feree's to ask how the business was doing. Frank played coy. He knew of Field's drinking problem but didn't want to tell the out-of-town owners.

"I can't find Fred," Guggenheim often complained to Frank. "What's going on down there?'

"I really don't know," Frank routinely replied. "I get in the truck in the mornings, make my rounds picking up raw materials at meat markets and return to the plant when there's nobody there. I just unload the truck and go home. Do the same thing the next day."

On his own initiative, because Fred Field was of no assistance, Frank had begun expanding his grease routes. He worked longer days but also increased the tonnage of animal wastes. That was a good sign for the owners, but they still were unhappy with a shortage of profits.

Agitated with the perpetually missing plant manager and getting no answers, Guggenheim and Jack Field showed up unannounced in Greensboro one Saturday morning in May 1936 with an employee, a Mr. Boyer, from their Norfolk rendering plant. They introduced the stranger to Frank as the new manager in Greensboro. They fired Field's brother Fred on the spot.

The Norfolk employee looked over the Greensboro production plant and had a quick reaction. "Forget it," Boyer told the plant owners.

Boyer said he would not accept the new assignment. Greensboro was too small a city and the plant was too dumpy for him to be part of either. Field and Guggenheim had a business on the verge of bankruptcy and no manager. But they had the energetic young worker named Stanley Frank.

"Well, let's just give the kid the plant," Guggenheim said to Field, referring to his nephew Frank. "If he fails, we haven't lost much because we don't have much anyway. And maybe it will work. He might make it."

Field agreed, having little other choice. At age 21, four months after arriving in Greensboro, Stanley Frank became manager of a rendering plant that wasn't making any money and had little hope at that moment of ever making much.

As manager, though, Frank received one perk: a car, such as it was. Company owners bought a used, beat up Chevrolet and gave it to their new manager as his personal vehicle. Hardly high-class transportation, it was still better than driving the grease truck at night.

"I was the kid with a plant to run," Frank said of that Saturday's events. "So on Monday morning, I became plant manager, meaning I needed to stay at the plant to oversee the production. I had to hire a truck driver on Sunday night."

Frank remembered a former plant employee, a hard worker, who had been fired by an intoxicated Fred Field even though he had been one of the company's best and most dedicated employees.

"Want a job?" Frank asked Tom Morris, who was sitting at home, still unemployed.

"Yes, sir, I sure do," Morris replied. The next

morning Morris took over Frank's routes and Frank took control of the production process.

Morris looked considerably less than dapper with dirty overalls and tobacco juice staining both sides of his mouth. But Frank surmised that an appearance like that didn't much matter on grease and animal parts routes.

Frank took over his management duties for $16 a week (and the used car), a full dollar above his $15 a week starting salary from four months earlier. "That's about all they could afford under the circumstances," Frank explained. Guggenheim also promised that he would give Frank some equity in company plants outside Greensboro and pledged that Frank would inherit Carolina By-Products Company at Guggenheim's death. That promise was enough of an incentive for Frank to devote his energies to the task of turning the plant into a profitable enterprise.

Frank did receive a small percentage of ownership in plants in other cities, but Guggenheim never fulfilled his promise that his nephew would inherit the Greensboro operation. Frank inherited only a small part of Carolina By-Products when his uncle died; Guggenheim gave most of the assets to other relatives, none interested in or connected with the company. Frank later said that while the broken promise from his uncle personally hurt him, it did not surprise him.

Promises aside, however, Frank was determined to improve the profit picture for two reasons. First, he wanted to prove to himself and his Uncle Herbert that he could do it. Second, he wanted to get Guggenheim off his back. "He was very hard and overbearing on me like he was with others," Frank said of his uncle. "He was trying to develop me, but he wasn't sure I could handle the job. He was nice to his wife and respected in Washington as a businessman, but he was generally grumpy and overbearing in dealing with people. His outer shell was pretty rough."

Frank did, in fact, begin showing a profit, slim though it was, in the early years of management. In lieu of salary increases, his Uncle Herbert kept his promise to Frank and arranged for his nephew to get a small ownership share of company plants outside Greensboro.

Token salary increases came over time. Three years after assuming responsibility of running the Greensboro plant, Frank's salary had climbed from $16 to $40 a week. That was his pay when he was married in 1939.

Low pay and low profits were not Frank's only concerns when he was handed responsibility for Carolina By-Products. He also had to fight a lawsuit by neighbors of the plant and a charge that dead animals at the plant had inflicted disease on local cattle herds.

In 1935, shortly before Frank came to Greensboro, residents in the southeast section of town filed the legal claim against the company, alleging that odors from the plant were disrupting their lives and waste runoff was contaminating their wells. They sued for $25,000. "I wasn't in town when the suit was filed, but I heard about it when I got here and had to deal with it," Frank explained.

Meanwhile, dairyman Tom Pemberton on Alamance Church Road, east of the city, was claiming his cattle had contracted and were dying from the deadly anthrax disease resulting from infected animals shipped in from the Midwest and slaughtered at the city's abattoir before Carolina By-Products recycled waste parts.

Gruff Uncle Herbert gave his plant manager nephew a simple directive. "Lose that lawsuit and you're out of a job," he said with conviction.

"It was a tough time," Frank said of those years. "The lawsuit was serious. People were unhappy with the plant and its perceived reputation. It was actually the city that was causing a lot of the odors from the abattoir, but we got cracked with the blame. To make matters worse, I was a damned Yankee who wasn't from around here and had not been a part of the local community."

Those episodes, though difficult at the time, were also great learning experiences for the young rendering plant manager. He concluded early on that if he ever expected to be a success in Greensboro, he had to show a willingness to be supportive of and work with local residents. The experience taught him to become involved. It was then and there that he became an active participant in the life of his adopted city.

Carolina By-Products lost the civil suit filed by the neighbors near the end of the 1930s. But by the time it was settled, the company had begun showing a regular profit and Uncle Herbert was at least somewhat satisfied. Frank's job was safe, despite the threat from Guggenheim about losing the court fight.

Frank adopted a plan for incorporating himself into the southeast Greensboro community. And to prevent future legal actions, he started programs to help keep the air and water supplies as clean as possible. When he added workers, he hired them from that section of town. After Frank was married in 1939, he routinely stopped by neighborhood homes to buy eggs and vegetables. He likely could have found eggs as fresh and cheap in the grocery store, but he felt it was important to give business to and show concern for those in the area of his plant.

He and his friend and fellow businessman Vernon Hodgin, who owned a roofing company in the area, became leaders in the South Greensboro Exchange Club and South Greensboro Businessman's Club. The Exchange Club purchased a home on Asheboro Street for use as a recreation center for young people in the neighborhood.

The neighborhood and the clubhouse were initially segregated. Frank and Hodgin felt that was wrong and worked to include racial minorities from nearby neighborhoods. Some of the association members objected, but Frank's policy of openness prevailed and the recreation center was integrated.

In his first years in Greensboro, Frank's community efforts were limited to the area south of the railroad tracks that divided the city. Then he moved to the other side of the tracks and joined the American Business Club, made up mostly of small business owners from closer to the center of town. "I went from one organization to another," Frank said. "I devoted as much time as I could to the community."

One club Frank was not asked to join was the M&M Club. That was the semi-secretive club made up exclusively of the wealthy corporate owners and officers in the city during the decades of the middle 1900s. The club met in the basement of the O. Henry Hotel, always behind closed doors for poker playing, liquor drinking and deal making.

"That club was far too high brow for me to participate," Frank said. "It was strictly upper end. I had no association with that crowd at that point."

As Frank's reputation grew within the southeast Greensboro community, so did company profits. He still was not making a big salary, but he was able to turn profits into expansion efforts. Under his leadership and guidance, Carolina By-Products opened a rendering plant in Gastonia in 1946 and purchased existing plants in Asheville and in Sanford in the years from 1948 to 1952. Other plants would be started or purchased during the next 30 years.

In 1948, Greensboro City Councilman Ben Cone, who a year later was elected mayor, made it known it was time for the city to exit the abattoir business for at least two reasons. The cattle market had opened up for individual producers and Cone decreed the city had no business being in that business any longer, if it ever had. With the support of company owners, Frank arranged for Carolina By-Products to purchase the city's abattoir for $30,000, immediately leasing it to next door neighbor Curtis Brothers (later Curtis Packing) Company.

But other changes were in order. It was also in 1948 that Frank's Uncle Herbert decided to sell the Washington, D.C., rendering plant as part of the final settlement of the Milton Hopfenmaier estate. He asked Frank to help in the negotiations. The sale was successful to a rendering company in New York. But things didn't work out as well for Frank's father Hugo, who found himself without a job after the new owners brought in their own plant manager.

Frank offered his father a job in North Carolina, an offer that was readily accepted. Hugo Frank moved to Gastonia and worked as a solicitor of new business at that plant for more than a dozen years until his retirement in 1960. Frank said his father was a "great talker who could smooze with new customers" and was good for business. Hugo Frank died in Gastonia on August 6, 1962. He never worked directly for his son, instead reporting to the plant manager at the Gaston County facility. But it was a safe bet that his job was safe as long as he wanted it.

In the fall of 1953 Frank encountered another crisis, one he certainly had never anticipated. In the span of less than one week in October that year, Jack Field and Herbert Guggenheim both died. Field succumbed to the ravages of leukemia and Guggenheim died of a massive heart attack. Almost overnight, Frank suddenly faced two agonizing choices: working for new owners or searching for another job. His third option was to become his own boss at Carolina By-Products, despite the debt and uncertainties that he knew he would face. With abundant anxiety and hope, he chose that route.

During the early lean years when Guggenheim and Field couldn't afford pay increases for Frank, they awarded him ten percent of the ownership in rendering plants in Sanford, Asheville, and Gastonia. But he was never given stock in Carolina By-Products, which he had managed successfully.

"I was a very small minority shareholder in the company plants outside Greensboro when the two principal owners died so suddenly so close together. I had to make a move or most likely be out," Frank said.

Once Frank realized that his Uncle Herbert's promise of bequeathing him Carolina By-Products would never become reality, he took a bold step, one that he didn't relish because he despised debt. At the time, however, he concluded that debt as a company owner was better than no debt and no job. In December 1953, Frank arranged loans of roughly $1 million from banks and from his Aunt Sara, widow of Uncle Herbert Guggenheim. He became the principal owner of Carolina By-Products Company, Inc., after buying the shares that his other relatives had inherited from Guggenheim.

When Frank bought the company, he awarded ten percent ownership to each of two men who helped him make the acquisition. To show his appreciation for their help, he gave Washington lawyer Louis Denit and Washington accountant J. H. Verkouteren the partial ownership at the time of purchase, but later bought back their shares, giving each man a handsome profit. "They were both essential to helping me buy the company and they were good and honest men," Frank said. "I felt they deserved a chance to turn a profit if I succeeded." He, of course, did succeed.

Frank paid off his debt on his established schedule. That was the last time he ever needed to borrow money at his company. His best years would lie ahead.

5

Romancing Dorothy

There was no yellow brick road ahead when Stanley Frank stepped off the train in Greensboro on that cold, breezy morning in late January 1936. But there was a Dorothy and the makings of a fairytale romance and marriage that had already lasted more than 60 years at the beginning of the 21st century.

Whatever success Frank achieved from his long hours and lean years in the rendering business, much of the credit comes from his successes at home. There Dorothy Goss Frank maintained a steady hand and firm control during years of nagging family illnesses and decades of extended family care. Her role was no less important than his has been in the family's ultimate success and philanthropy.

"She's pretty special," Frank said with a sparkle in his eye, describing his long-time marriage partner. "She's a wonderful lady, the most unselfish person I have ever known, warm and considerate and tolerant. She's always thinking of other people first. She has all the good qualities you'd expect to find in a really fine person."

That's a tribute from the heart. One of the few times Frank ever spent lavishly on something he didn't really need was when he purchased his wife a sporty luxury vehicle that caused people to stop and look when she drove by. "Oh, it was a classy Lincoln, a Continental Mark III," Frank explained, grinning widely. "I wanted to do something special for Dorothy. She deserved it."

Her feelings for him are just as pronounced. "Stanley has been a wonderful husband and father and has done all that anyone could be expected to do," she said admiringly in her normally restrained way of speaking. "He worked hard and long to keep his business going, to make sure his family was cared for and secure. He is a good, caring person."

Shortly after their marriage in the spring of 1939, they began calling each other "Butch," which each considers a term of endearment. That nickname has lasted over six decades.

Rather unromantically, the need for a section of pipe and fittings at Carolina By-Products is what started their relationship.

During the first years of his business career in Greensboro, Frank spent many hours patching up worn machine parts. He often worked seven days a week as he struggled to pacify his generally ornery boss, Uncle Herbert, and turn a profit by processing animal wastes into consumer goods ranging from soap and other household products to poultry and hog feed. He had little free time to meet people and even less to socialize outside the office.

Revenue was slim, equipment was flimsy, and

repairs were frequent, usually done by company personnel as a cost-saving measure. In February 1938, two years after he got to town, Frank made his way to a wholesale plumbing store in search of a pipe and fittings for cookers at the rendering plant he managed.

On that day, looking for parts at the cheapest price, Frank met Henry Goss, the gregarious plumbing shop owner with a big heart and a house full of unmarried sisters.

Determining in the initial meeting that Frank, a fellow Jew, was a personable and pleasant fellow who would likely enjoy meeting his family, Goss invited him to visit that Saturday night.

A shy and skinny 23-year-old Frank put on his one set of dress clothes. As had been his habit for more than six decades, he showed up early. It didn't take him long to realize there was a lot more to the Goss family than interesting parents and plumbing parts. Unbeknownst to Frank, Henry Goss had nine single sisters. The first of the nine Goss daughters to come downstairs that night to meet the guest was Dorothy.

It was a meeting embedded for life in Frank's memory. "The whole family was there, with a lot of pretty young women among the daughters, but I picked Dorothy out," he said. "Right then, I began thinking of her as a girlfriend." A week later, Frank asked Dorothy out to dinner for their first official date. From that day forward, he never dated another woman.

His infatuation, however, was more pronounced than hers was.

While he was smitten on the spot that night during the family introductions, her feelings were a bit longer evolving. "Oh, I thought he was a nice person when we met," Dorothy Frank said, "but I wasn't personally interested in him at first. My family, though, thought he was really special and my mother loved him from the start."

Dorothy Goss Frank, on her wedding day, March 5, 1939.

Dorothy would not allow herself to fall too fast, as he did, because of her strong feelings about people with his geographical background. "She told me later she had always said she would never marry a damned Yankee," Frank said with a grin.

Pretty soon, however, Dorothy abandoned her broad-brush views about people from New York and adopted the view of the rest of the Goss family. She fell in love with Stanley Frank.

From that first meeting in February 1938, their relationship grew stronger with each date, which was as frequent as Frank could find the time and cash. They were married a year later, in March 1939, in a ceremony that opened the door to a future well beyond the power of their combined beliefs at the time.

The Frank/Goss marriage in Greensboro at Temple Emanuel, although not extravagant, was a joyous occasion, with one notable exception. Because Frank's father was present, his mother refused to attend, passing up on the chance to witness her only son's wedding. Her continued ill feelings toward her former husband were so strong that she didn't want to be in his presence, even for their son's marriage.

Three days after the wedding, on a bitterly cold, snowy weekend in a car with no heater, Frank drove his new bride to New Jersey to meet her new mother-in-law.

Frank and his bride spent their first night of marriage at the Virginian Hotel in Lynchburg, before continuing northward, spending their second night in the DuPont Hotel in Wilmington, Delaware. From there, they made it to New Jersey, fighting cold weather and bad roads, to spend one day with his mother before heading for the Ambassador Hotel in Atlantic City. They spent a third night there before heading back south to Washington, D.C., where Frank's employers had asked him to attend a meeting.

It was a trip that neither Frank nor his wife will ever forget. Snow, sleet and freezing rain made driving hazardous, but Frank had a schedule to meet. Because of the absence of a heater or defroster in Frank's Chevrolet, Dorothy held her hands against the inside windshield to warm it enough to melt frozen condensation so her husband could see the road. Though foul weather made them late for the Washington meeting, Frank was chastised by his Uncle Herbert for not arriving on time. "We were lucky to get there at all," Frank said. "Dorothy darn near froze her hands on that ice-coated windshield. That's the only way we made it."

That was just one of many times through the years that Dorothy Frank was ready when her husband needed a helping hand.

Jacob Goss, a native of Germany, Dorothy Frank's father, a scrap metal dealer and devout Orthodox Jew, who gave up his studies to become a rabbi when he met his future wife, Anna. This photograph was made in the summer of 1941.

•

One year and one month after Stanley Frank was born on June 7, 1914, as the second child and only son to a Manhattan couple whose marriage was collapsing, Dorothy Goss was born on July 9, 1915, into a solid, close-knit family in Berryville, Virginia. Berryville, a town of 1,100 residents, was 10 miles from Winchester, an hour west of Washington, D.C. She was the sixth of nine daughters in a family that also included two sons.

Both families were Jewish. But while Frank's parents, Hugo and Adele Frank, did not practice or show much concern for their religious faith, before or after their marriage breakup, the Goss family was just the opposite. Dorothy's parents, Jacob and Anna Goss, were devout in their beliefs and devotion to Judaism and were determined that their children follow their lead.

Jacob's father had been an Orthodox rabbi in Germany and his mother had insisted her son do likewise. Jacob complied with her wishes, at least temporarily, and as a teenager in Germany in the early 1890s, began his course of study for full-time Orthodox synagogue work.

Then in the late 1890s he met Anna Wilson while both his and her parents were living in Lithuania.

"My father always said she was the most beautiful woman he had ever seen," Dorothy Frank said of her father's description of her mother. "He was devoted to his faith and also devoted to her."

But Anna issued an ultimatum and Jacob had to make a choice. She would never, she said, marry a rabbi and would never marry a man who would not agree to come to the United States. Jacob Goss did not take long to decide his future. He ended his rabbinical training at age 18, went to Berlin for a short while and then came to the United States with plans to bring his future wife to his new country. Like Dorothy when she met Stanley, Anna was not initially as willing as Jacob to begin a new life, especially one in a foreign land — even though she had said that's what she wanted.

Jacob Goss came to America shortly after the turn to the 20th century. Anna came 14 months later. "My mother always did take her time in de-

Anna Wilson Goss, Dorothy Frank's mother, 1941. As a young woman in Lithuania where her parents lived, Anna promised to marry Jacob Goss if he would come to America and abandon his plans to become a rabbi.

ciding things," Dorothy Frank said with a smile. The couple married in Philadelphia, in the first decade of the 1900s, and Jacob began searching for a career to support his family, which had begun to grow almost immediately.

He headed west to survey the landscape, making stops along the way, but the farther he went the less he liked what he saw. When he reached Sandusky, Ohio, he had seen enough; he turned around and headed back east. A friend from his native Germany had settled in West Virginia and recommended to Goss that he consider settling somewhere along the East Coast. The Goss family chose the tiny town of Berryville, Virginia, as the place for their family home; Jacob began his career as a scrap metal and junk dealer, buying and selling used machine parts, and running a general store.

But even though Jacob Goss had abandoned earlier plans to become a rabbi, he didn't give up his active religious faith, even as one of the few Jews in Berryville. He admonished his family to remain dedicated in their devotion to Judaism as he daily practiced his Orthodox beliefs. His wife and children partially complied, but none was so devout as the patriarch in adhering to his strict dietary and religious rules.

The family settled down to what they thought would be a lifelong stay in Berryville until oldest son Henry, the second child, contracted inflammatory rheumatism in the mid 1920s and a doctor advised his parents to move to a different climate. The family chose Greensboro, with drier weather as well as a potentially wider market for scrap metal.

The family first rented a home on Asheboro

Street. Jacob Goss later purchased his first home at 200 South Elam Avenue, not far from the center of the city. The family continued to increase in size as Jacob Goss' business steadily grew. But with 11 children to clothe and feed, the economic status of the household never reached beyond middle class. Though Jacob Goss was a respected businessman of the city, he never reached the higher end of the economic ladder and never became a part of the social scene, limiting himself to his scrap metal business and his Orthodox Judaism.

Goss never allowed himself to break from his dogmatic religious beliefs. He ate only kosher meals and declined invitations to dine with his children as adults because they did not follow his strict dietary practices.

"He always told me he had followed what he felt was right for him in his beliefs, but we were of a different generation and it was all right for us to do what we felt was acceptable," Dorothy Frank said of her father. Anna Goss would prepare kosher meals at home for her husband, then visit her children and dine on other meals in their homes.

Jacob Goss died in Greensboro on July 20, 1960, at the age of 79, eight months after the death on November 16, 1959, of his wife Anna, who died at the age of 77.

•

In the 1940s in Greensboro, there was no Orthodox or conservative synagogue. Religious services at Temple Emanuel, a reformed house of worship, were divided, with reformed Jews meeting at designated hours and the more conservative believers at another time. When the original conservative synagogue, Beth David, was built in 1947, Dorothy Frank was asked to join that house of worship because of her father's strong conservative faith.

She declined, saying her allegiance was to the more moderate Temple Emanuel, where she had been a member her adult life and where she and her two sons were married. She also felt her husband would not be comfortable in the more conservative religious setting. He, in fact, had no religious affiliation when they were married; Dorothy brought him into the re-formed Jewish faith.

Frank's mother also had come from a strong religious background in Germany, but she and her sisters had faded from their faith after coming to the United States. "I always felt that was a sad aspect of their lives," Dorothy Frank said, "but that's just the way it was. Stanley grew up without any religious teaching or training. He became part of my faith only after we were married."

Through his wife's urging, Frank became a viable member of Temple Emanuel and has served as president of the congregation even though he has never been confirmed into the Jewish faith and isn't a regular attendee at weekly services. The Franks' son Barry has also served as president of the temple.

"I don't have a tendency to be very publicly religious even today and have become somewhat less active in recent years," Frank said of his approach to his faith. "But I do have a great belief in God. I pray privately regularly."

•

Stanley Frank and Dorothy Goss found time for frequent dates during their one-year courtship in 1938, although most of their hours together were spent at her home or at inexpensive restaurants. His weekly salary was $40 as the rendering plant manager and her income was $12.50 a week as a jewelry store clerk. Their favorite place to go out was Helen's, a popular but unpretentious steak restaurant and tavern west of town, on Old Highway 421, near what is now the regional airport. That is where he had taken her on their first date the week after they met.

Helen's, highly regarded by Greensboro's elite Irving Park crowd, was recognized for its good food and strict rules that allowed only selected customers inside. A sort of membership club without dues, the clientele was limited to whomever sole proprietor and self-styled bouncer Helen decided to admit.

Dorothy Goss' brother Henry had been involved in some business dealings with Helen, so he and his family were always welcomed at her restaurants.

In reality, Helen's was a speakeasy in which diners could purchase alcoholic drinks despite local laws prohibiting such sales. The facility was equipped with a small window in the front door that allowed for screening of customers. Although she served alcohol, proprietor Helen had an unbending rule against those who showed up with evidence of drinking. Customers could, and occasionally did, become intoxicated inside, but if they arrived in that condition, they were turned away. Helen's rules were rock-solid, no exceptions.

Helen's iron-fisted owner was Helen Anderson, a former fan dancer who had operated an illegal drink house in Texas during Prohibition days. An oft-wed woman, her last spouse was a much younger Larry Anderson, who worked at Helen's as a piano player.

After Helen closed her own eatery and drink house, she moved to the Embassy Club at Sedgefield, where she continued her tradition of good food and strict rules. "She was a very domineering woman," said Greensboro Realtor Charles (Buddy) Weill Jr., who remembered Helen from the Embassy Club days. "When you met her, you sort of felt like asking 'May I?' when you wanted something. When you called for dinner reservations, you tended to ask if it was okay. She had a really tough façade, but she was kind and considerate to friends. She did nice things for people who were nice to her."

Helen's loyalty to her customers was made clear in her final days. Fatally ill with cancer and knowing her end was near, Helen hired an ambulance to drive her across town; there she stopped at homes of long-time customers in Irving Park to tell them goodbye. She also directed the ambulance driver to make a final drive through Sedgefield so she could see one last time the site of the Embassy Club. Helen died the next day.

Dorothy Frank recalled one occasion that illustrated Helen's defiant attitude against inebriated customers, regardless of status.

The governor of Pennsylvania knocked at Helen's speakeasy door following attendance at a football game in Chapel Hill. He appeared more than a little intoxicated, so Helen told him to get lost.

He wasn't pleased, to say the least. "Do you know who I am," he shouted through the little window on the door. "I'm the governor of Pennsylvania."

"I don't give a damn who you are," Helen responded. "You're drunk and you're not coming in my restaurant." The agitated governor may have found dinner in Greensboro that night, but he didn't find it at Helen's.

•

Stanley Frank won Dorothy Goss' heart and her father's permission to marry after 13 months of courting. Rabbi Frederick Rypins at Temple Emanuel married them on March 5, 1939.

When Frank announced his plans to marry, his bosses bumped his salary to $45 a week. After the wedding and the eventful trip to New Jersey and Washington, the couple moved into Country Club Apartments on North Elm Street. The rent was $50 a month, with no laundry facilities. The apartments were among the city's finest. Most of the non-working wives spent rainy days at bridge games.

Dorothy Frank chose not to join the social scene at the apartments, declaring the hours of bridge and gossip a waste of time. "They all thought I was kind of odd because I wouldn't sit around all day in a negligee and talk as they did," she said. Among their closest friends in the apartment complex, owned at the time by Jefferson Standard president Julian Price, were Jack and Leah Tannenbaum, also newlyweds, also Jewish. Jack Tannenbaum would later become the Franks' physician.

Fourteen months of life in the apartment among the social set of the city was enough for the Franks. "Stanley was still making only $45 a week, but we figured that because his company furnished him a car and gasoline we would be able to buy a small house," Dorothy Frank said.

They were able to afford their own place but just barely — and it took a used kitchen stove and refrigerator to swing the deal.

The Franks, after ruling out most houses in the city's northwest side for lack of funds, found a home they felt they could afford on Hendrix Street in old Fisher Park, between North Elm and Church streets, and put down a $100 deposit that virtually wiped out their bank account. Before the contract was signed, however, they learned of another house going on the market around the corner at 809 Olive Street.

"We both loved the Olive Street house more," Dorothy Frank explained, "but we didn't have money enough for the purchase price because we were about to lose the $100 deposit on the Hendrix Street house. We didn't know what to do."

Postal inspector C.H. McQueen, who was being transferred out of town and was selling his Olive Street home through Realtor Charles Weill Sr., wanted to make a quick deal and realized how much the Franks wanted his residence. McQueen and Weill offered a compromise. Weill told the prospective buyers he had been authorized to knock $100 off McQueen's asking price of $4,000 to compensate for their earlier deposit on the other home. McQueen also knew the couple had no appliances, so for another $50 he tossed in his used kitchen stove and refrigerator.

That sealed the deal. For $3,950 Stanley and Dorothy Frank bought the Olive Street home with six rooms, one bath, a front porch, and a used refrigerator and stove. They assumed their first mortgage, financing the home through the previous owner, at the going interest rate at the time, May 1940, of four percent.

The home, one of the smaller Fisher Park residences, had a central heating system from a coal-fired furnace and a coal-burning stove for heating water. Both the furnace and stove were in the basement. Because her husband was away for long hours at his job, Dorothy Frank literally shoveled coal to keep the home and water warm.

The Frank family grew by two sons as well as a mother-in-law over the next decade. While life was mostly tranquil, there were some traumatic as well as sad days ahead, including death and a life-threatening illness.

Within months after purchasing their first home, Stanley Frank's mother moved in, not for a visit but for the remainder of her life. Adele Loeb Frank lived with her son, daughter-in-law and two grandchildren for 21 years. Stanley and Dorothy Frank gave up their largest bedroom for his mother's use and they used a smaller bedroom for themselves during their ten years in the Olive Street home.

On October 1, 1941, Dorothy Frank gave birth to premature identical twin sons in Wesley Long

Adele Loeb Frank, Stanley Frank's mother, in the late 1950s. Mrs. Frank worked as a seamstress and beautician in order to keep her children together following her divorce in 1914. She lived in Greensboro with Stanley and Dorothy Frank and their two children for more than 20 years.

81

Hospital. William Frank was born first, barely alive, six weeks short of full term. He weighed a miniscule two pounds and 14 ounces. His twin brother was born moments later, even more fragile, lighter and weaker.

The second twin's lungs were so filled with mucus that he was unable to survive the congestion on his own and doctors were unable to clear his breathing passages. This baby died after a 14-hour struggle, still unnamed. Dorothy Frank was never allowed to hold, even to see her second twin, as doctors worked to save the life of the firstborn by, among other actions, wrapping him in blankets covered by hot water bottles to provide warmth.

Doctors later told the parents they had never seen a child as weak and tiny as Bill Frank survive, even as they fought to keep him alive. To help ensure survival during the first weeks of her son's life, Dorothy Frank was required to provide breast milk each day from a sterilized pump doctors had allowed her to take home while she left the infant behind in the hospital. Her husband daily delivered the breast milk to the hospital where Baby Bill remained for six weeks of close monitoring. "Nurses started calling Stanley the milk man," Dorothy Frank said.

The Franks took their tiny son home only after he reached a weight of five pounds and two ounces, six weeks after birth. Even then, he was so frail that his parents were required to wear masks in his presence to avoid possibly spreading germs. For the first few months of his life, they had to weigh him each day, before and after each feeding, and report his progress to doctors. Her fear of germs was so great that Dorothy Frank sterilized diaper pins after each use.

The child, with strong will, survived, only to encounter another ordeal that almost took his life at age six. As a first grade student in 1948 when the polio epidemic spread across Greensboro and other parts of the country, Bill Frank began to have problems swallowing and difficulty breathing. Medical tests proved his parents' worst fear; their son had contracted a variety of polio that was worse than the more common paralyzing form. It was often fatal.

Bill Frank's type of polio, Bulbar, was the most serious form, resulting from damage to nerve cells in the brain stem and affecting swallowing and moving of eyes, tongue, face and neck as well as body fluids. Recovery was based on immediate detection, proper care and complete rest.

The child was hospitalized for four months, from April until August 1948. During that hospital stay, one reckless nurse burned his skin by applying hot packs with temperatures near the scalding range, inflicting more pain.

Dorothy Frank sat each day for hours beside her son's hospital bed, watching his throat to see if she could detect any swallowing motion. Nurses didn't have time for such precise observation because of the high volume of polio patients. After months of inability to swallow any liquids or even his own saliva, surviving from intravenous fluids, Bill Frank swallowed a teaspoon of water. It was, his mother said, a joyous occasion. He began his recovery, one teaspoon of water at a time.

"He was so hungry and thin, but he couldn't swallow and couldn't eat on his own for many months," his mother said. Even after returning home, he was kept in isolation behind a glass enclosure to ward off germs from other family members. His mother was taught to perform proper daily exercises to help her son regain his strength. She was also taught medical treatments to aid in his recovery, including therapeutically tying his feet to the bed to keep them from becoming deformed.

As an adult, Bill Frank doesn't remember much about his experience with the near fatal disease, except the constant hunger and the pain of burns from the overzealous nurse who wouldn't listen to his pleas that she was hurting him. There are few permanent scars, only a slight, almost unrecognizable limp, and an occasional temporary swallowing problem.

Four years after Bill Frank's traumatic birth and two years before his bout with polio, a second son, Barry, was born on September 12, 1945. His health problems didn't compare to the seriousness of his older brother's, but they were not to be taken lightly by his parents.

During delivery of the second son, a nurse, who had not expected the birth so rapidly, attempted to hold the mother's legs together until a doctor arrived. That trauma to the newborn was later determined to be a partial cause of epileptic seizures.

"That's the way it happens," Dorothy Frank said. "Someone makes a mistake and somebody else pays for it the rest of their life." As an adult, Barry Frank controls the seizures with a daily dose of medicine. His experiences, however, have prompted him to become an active participant in epileptic awareness and treatment efforts. He has served as a member of the board of directors of the Epilepsy Foundation of North Carolina.

Dorothy Frank's efforts at restoring and protecting the health of her two sons has also extended to her own and her husband's lives. She credits medical examinations at the Greenbrier Clinic in White Sulfur Springs, West Virginia, with possibly saving both their lives.

Doctors at the Greenbrier, where the Franks make annual visits for physical exams, discovered a lump in her breast during a mammography, a lump that had gone undetected in tests in Greensboro. Doctors there also discovered polyps in Frank's colon that would, they said, almost certainly have become malignant if left untreated. Surgery in Greensboro resolved both those problems. Physicians at the Greenbrier are known for the quality of their medical examinations, but they don't perform surgery, leaving that to patients' doctors back in their hometowns.

"Doctors in Greensboro were amazed that [Greenbrier physicians] were able to find those lumps in me because they were so tiny," Dorothy Frank explained. "And our doctors said they never would have caught those polyps in Stanley because they didn't do the same kinds of tests here. The pathologists in Greensboro called the Greenbrier and thanked the medical people there. I think they saved both our lives."

That polyp surgery is one of a series of potentially fatal medical problems Stanley Frank has encountered. He once was near death following complications from a botched operation on his appendix and again after contracting lockjaw because of infection from a hand wound suffered at work. "I guess I'm lucky to be alive," Frank said shortly before his 86th birthday. "There have been several times during the 1940s and 1950s when I wasn't sure I would be alive for long."

At age 85, Frank, a former smoker, learned from doctors at the Greenbrier of a spot on one lung. Since that time, he has made regular trips to Johns Hopkins Hospital for tests, but surgery had not been required or even recommended into his 87th year.

•

After a decade in their small Olive Street home, Stanley and Dorothy Frank determined that with two growing sons and a mother-in-law at home, they needed larger quarters. The rendering plant still wasn't as profitable as it could have been or as Frank wanted, but it was doing steadily better and he felt comfortable in seeking a larger home.

They searched for homes in the Starmount section not far from downtown where they lived and in the west toward Guilford College. They didn't like most of what they saw and couldn't afford the few they did like. A few friends advised them against purchasing one of those "expensive" Starmount homes.

Their real estate friend Buddy Weill, whose father had helped close the sale of their Olive Street home, told them about a home in the community of Sedgefield, at the time in 1950 considered far out in the country off High Point Road. Sedgefield was then evolving as a neighborhood of established Greensboro families or those on the way up the economic ladder, although at the time it was still much closer to the series of dairy farms that it once was than it was to the upscale residential area it would later become.

The Sedgefield home that Weill had recommended was on Alamance Road, one of the main streets into the development. Contractor George W. Kane had built it in 1928 and 1929. The local architect was Harry

Barton, one of the designers of Greensboro's downtown upscale First Presbyterian Church. The original owner was Dr. E.J. Woodhouse, head of the History Department at the University of North Carolina in Chapel Hill; his wife, Chase Going Woodhouse, was the vocational and job placement director from 1928 until 1934 at what was then Woman's College in Greensboro, later the University of North Carolina at Greensboro.

Woodhouse paid $4,000 for the lot that faces the 17th fairway at the Sedgefield Golf Course and paid the Kane Company $24,274 for the home, excluding architect fees and landscaping.

The Woodhouses had two children and a live-in mother-in-law, just as the Franks. After the Woodhouse couple separated, the house was rented by various university faculty members for several years and eventually sold to Shirley and Ruth Claire Hurt. At Shirley Hurt's death, his widow reluctantly put the house on the market.

The Franks looked at the house several times. Frank initially wasn't overly fond of the English Tudor style. He was also skeptical because the home had been on the market for more than a year. "What's wrong with it?" he asked Weill.

Even with a dirt driveway, no bathroom on the first floor and a laundry room in the basement, it offered much of what the family needed. It had ample room for the Frank sons and their grandmother. Convinced by Weill, whom he trusted, that there was no problem with the home, Frank made an offer on January 16, 1950.

Frank's purchase offer of $27,500 was accepted after several months of intense negotiating, amid his growing impatience with the owner's inability to decide on a closing date. The family moved in on June 15, 1950. The county tax value of the home when the Frank's bought it was $10,780 and the annual property tax bill was $127.20.

Half a century and several renovations later, the house was valued at approximately $750,000. In their estate planning when they die or move, the Franks have arranged for their home to become the property of Guilford College, where they have donated several million dollars toward the school's development.

While Frank seemed to get a good deal on the purchase, because his cost was less than the original construction price of the house and land, it wasn't an easy step for him and his family. Frank didn't want another home mortgage, so he borrowed $15,000 from a Washington bank where his company did business. This $15,000 he put with his savings in order to cover the $27,500 purchase price. He repaid the bank a simple interest loan rather than a mortgage, saving considerable interest costs.

The couple made various home improvements that included adding a garage and putting a bathroom and laundry room on the first floor while their sons were growing up and Frank's mother was living there. They considered building a smaller house on another lot they owned in Sedgefield after the sons left home and Frank's mother died on March 12, 1960.

They hired an architect and cleared the nearby lot for their planned third home. "One April evening we were walking across our lawn and Stanley turned to me and said, 'Dorothy, do you really want to leave here?' I quickly said, 'No,'" Dorothy Frank said. "He called the architect the next morning and canceled the construction plans. That was the end of it. We didn't want to move."

The Franks gave their vacant Sedgefield lot to son Barry and bought a second vacant lot there and gave it to son Bill. "We always wanted to treat each of the boys equally and fairly," their mother explained. "We want to live out our lives in this house. The boys have their own homes and have no need for this one, so we will give it to Guilford College to benefit their needs."

6

Healthy Profession & Life

The rendering industry may not be quite as old as prostitution, but it is a close second.

Rendering has been around since the earliest man began cooking raw meat over a campfire and saving the grease drippings for other uses.

Gaius Plinius Secundus (Pliny the Elder, A.D. 23-79) crafted the first crudely written record of rendering in the decades following the birth of Christ. He was a Roman soldier, scholar, historian, writer and naturalist. Pliny was also a curious experimenter and, intended or not, created what by the late 20th century had become part of the billion dollar rendering industry.

Among his unrefined methods of trial and error in finding new uses for leftover products, Pliny discovered that by mixing wood ashes and goat's tallow he could create an early form of a cleansing compound.

This cleansing compound, then, became the first

example of what is now known as soap. From that day until this, blending tallow from animal fats with other ingredients is the primary process for making soap. A joke sometimes heard among rendering industry representatives is that the next time you wash your hands, do the dishes or load the washing machine, you ought to give thanks to an animal.

Soap, however, is but one of many worthwhile consumer products to come from the rendering industry, which has made steady progress from those early days of Pliny through the Industrial Revolution, two World Wars and what could be called the Environmental Revolution of the late 1900s. Soap, of course, has changed from those early days, but it still starts the same with recycled animal fats and oils.

Hand and facial soap manufacturing at the beginning of the 21st century consumed less than 25 percent of the rendering industry production, down from more than 80 percent half a century earlier. As soap manufacturing decreased from animal fats and oils, animal feed production and industrial chemical uses increased, taking over the largest share of domestic consumption.

Rendering is recycling, plain and simple. It is the process, greatly oversimplified, of making something out of nothing. Water is boiled off animal byproducts through a heat transfer system. Tallow and grease remaining in the by-product are then removed through draining and compression.

In addition to the cleansing and other household uses as well as the creation of protein-rich ingredients for animal feed, a primary product from rendering is production of glycerin, a derivative of soap production. During World War II glycerin became an important product in the use of explosives and is still a major part of the health care industry for treating patients with heart disease.

Without the rendering industry, not only would household and industrial benefits be lacking, but also environmental problems would be greatly multiplied. The rendering industry, when performing as it should, works to waste no wastes.

Pliny and the *Homo sapiens* who came before him were the original recyclers. And just like the so-called second oldest profession, it has lasted and flourished.

In addition to soap and other cleansing products extracted from leftover inedible animal parts, consumers use a series of household goods from candles to cosmetics and paper to plastics that all originate from the rendering process. The better grades of tallow and grease are used in the manufacture of products used every day in most homes. Lower grades of animal by-products are used in the production of food for pets, poultry and hogs.

Diners in steak houses or chicken or pork restaurants may not think of it, but what they are consuming is but a mere portion of the animal that provided their meal. In most cases, no more than 60 percent — in some cases even less — of an animal is considered edible. That means that at least 40 percent is waste material. Without the rendering industry, that waste would go to landfills or be left somewhere as pollution, contamination or other health or environmental hazards.

The rendering industry recycles virtually 100 percent of all leftover animal parts for consumer products. Statistics show that the average person consumes

220 pounds of meat products each year, leaving a lot of leftovers from public eateries, butcher shops or commercial packing houses. The rendering industry collects and processes these materials in staggering volumes totaling more than 40 billion pounds a year with a total value of more than $2 billion. Two-thirds of the recycled goods are used as animal feed ingredients with another 10 to 15 percent used for chemical or soap products. The remainder is used in other products.

The rendering industry is also a major player in the export trade of the United States. Approximately 25 percent of all products produced by the rendering industry each year is shipped to and consumed in foreign lands.

This is the industry into which Stanley Frank became an increasingly significant player not long after arriving in Greensboro in 1936 and taking control of a rendering plant that at the time was not much more alive than some of the dead animals brought to the site.

Frank slowly but surely turned the plant around and in the process became one of Greensboro's best known and most respected citizens during the decades when he first worked there, then later owned and expanded the breadth and depth of operations. But he did not limit his business successes to transforming Carolina By-Products into a viable company.

He also became one of the nation's respected leaders in the rendering industry while serving as president of the National Renderers' Association and chairman of the Fats and Protein Research Foundation. Those national posts took him to the nation's capital as an industry lobbyist, to dozens of foreign countries as he worked to expand exports of recycled products and across the United States as he sought to improve the image and explain the importance of the rendering industry.

That industry has never been publicly regarded as a leading light because of the negative image it projects. Dealing with animal parts and olfactory obtrusiveness is not something many people strive to include on their resumes. Historically the industry has been considered a dirty and foul-smelling business, with some justification, and many operators of such plants shunned public involvement.

That has never been Frank's way of doing business. While he never touted his successful rendering plant ownership, he certainly never shunned from pride in his accomplishments. Continuously working to make things better in his professional performances, he developed a reputation among his peers across the country as visionary about environmental concerns, long before it became fashionable, and led the way in seeking better and cleaner ways of processing animal by-products.

"He was always ahead of the rest of us, ahead of his time when it came to vision in the industry," said Harold Oelbaum, a former business associate from New York who was an official in the national company that bought Frank's business in 1969. "He was very progressive, always looking for new products to produce and new, innovative ways of doing things. If others in the industry had listened to him they would have been better off."

For example, with the help of his engineer friend G.T. (Nick) Nickell, Frank designed and implemented a new washing process that helps cleanse the air. It uses high velocity sprays to greatly reduce odors and provide a more efficient manufacturing process. Frank was one of the first in the industry to adopt that method.

As far back as the 1940s, company records show that Frank was frequently reminding plant officials and workers of the importance of clean air and water coming from rendering processes. "Review your operations and make changes as necessary to avoid every possible way of unnecessary pollution of streams and the atmosphere," admonished one typical memo from Frank to Carolina By-Products managers in the middle 1940s. Also in that era Frank directed his delivery drivers to use sealed containers to reduce odors and leak-proof vehicles to eliminate pollution and contamination along the highways.

Locally, however, Frank established himself as a leader far beyond his rendering plant operations. He has served his community in dozens of volunteer capacities; his contributions in time and money have added considerably to the progress and successes of local institutions of higher education, the business sector, the regional airport, and professional sports, among other organizations.

He has done it all with little fanfare through years of quiet yet effective leadership, without ever seeking public office or the limelight. Frank began his local civic involvement in the early 1940s and steadily expanded his efforts over the next 60 years. He was still an active participant at the age of 87 at the beginning of the 21st century.

"He deserves a special award just for longevity, staying involved for so long and maintaining an interest in so many community projects," commented former Greensboro Mayor Jim Melvin. "He never seems to stop or even slow down."

But it hasn't always been easy and certainly wasn't during the earliest days of Frank's presence in Greensboro when he struggled to keep the rendering plant he managed afloat and, quite literally on two occasions, to keep himself alive.

Frank's challenges were enormous when he arrived from Richmond in Greensboro in early 1936 after fewer than 12 hours advance notice. He was young and lacked experience about rendering processes beyond picking up restaurant grease, collecting leftover animal parts from butcher shops and hauling dead farm animals to the rendering plant that had hired him in Richmond four months earlier.

In Greensboro, Frank initially worked 60 or more hours a week picking up restaurant leftovers and butcher shop animal parts on daily truck routes and then helping with processing the by-products in large cookers at the end of each day.

Four months later when Frank was named plant manager, the daily routine became even longer and more complex. He was responsible for all the rendering processes in addition to maintaining the truck routes and handling financial records.

That was his routine for the first several years. He worked to increase volumes of by-products to be processed, hired more people from the immediate neighborhood where his plant was located in southeast Greensboro and worked with a few nearby businessmen to improve the plight of young people in the area.

As World War II moved to the forefront of the nation's interest, the rendering industry became criti-

cally important. Glycerin, obtained from the manufacture of soap and production of tallow during the
cooking process, was considered by the government
as an important part of the country's defense system
and the rendering business was declared a critical and
essential industry for the war effort.

The rendering business is primarily what kept
Frank out of military service. During a physical examination for the Army, he learned he was partially
colorblind. But his role with the rendering plant caused
the military to determine he was more valuable producing a source of glycerin than he was carrying a
rifle. His connection to the rendering industry and his
reclassification to 3A (married with a child) deferred
his draft status until the war ended.

Because of the importance of the rendering process for production of glycerin, German prisoners of
war captured on the European battlefields were
brought to this country and used to help operate rendering plants and increase the supply of glycerin at
different parts of the United States. One of those plants
was in Norfolk, operated by the owners of Carolina
By-Products.

"Those prisoners were a cantankerous bunch,"
Frank said. "Hard to deal with."

The Norfolk tallow plant suffered a damaging
fire in the midst of the war and Frank was called on to
help. The raw materials that had been processed in
Norfolk had to be trucked to Richmond and Greensboro.

"We were up to our ears in work here," Frank
said, "but we had to help out because the fire closed
the Norfolk facility." Helping out meant driving from
Greensboro to Norfolk, loading trucks with meat mar-

ket and packinghouse by-products and hauling the material to Greensboro for processing.

The smell was enough to melt an olfactometer. "It was a miserable situation," Frank said, recalling the trips and the odors. "Summertime in 90 degree temperatures we were hauling that raw material for five or six hours in open bed trucks from Norfolk down to Greensboro." Workers in Greensboro then unloaded the raw material from trucks into wheelbarrows and dumped the material into cooking vats.

There was nothing pleasant about that experience. Even as volume continued to increase along with the smell, Frank began looking for a better, more efficient way as the summer heat bore down on him and his workers. He and mechanic Ralph Nelson devised an improved production system, but it cost Frank the tip of one finger and put him in the hospital with a life-threatening illness.

Labor was scarce at the time in 1944 because so many of the able bodied workers in Greensboro, as elsewhere, had been shipped off to war. Frank and his mechanic Nelson designed a belt conveyor that would allow mechanized movement of the by-products. Carolina Steel Company in Greensboro built the conveyor but Frank and Nelson decided to personally install it.

"Ralph (Nelson) was drilling on the steel and I was holding one section. The drill slipped and cut off the end of this finger," Frank said, holding up his right hand, middle finger.

Frank wrapped his bleeding finger in a towel and drove himself to Wesley Long Hospital to get the wound stitched. He was pleased to see Dr. William Norment, a widely known and respected local surgeon, in the emergency room and felt relieved that Dr.

Norment treated the wound and sent him back to work. His relief would not last long.

Ten days later, Frank's jaw muscles began to tighten. He had trouble opening his mouth and swallowing. His fever shot skyward. Dizziness and headaches set in. Other muscles began to spasm. He had contracted tetanus, more commonly known as lockjaw. Lockjaw is a disease caused by dust and dirt in open wounds. Affecting muscles, it is a serious illness but treatable with antitoxins. The illness was brought on because Dr. Norment had failed to give Frank a tetanus shot when he sewed the finger wound and infection had begun to poison his body.

"There was plenty of tetanus vaccine available because of the war and I don't know why the doctor didn't give me a shot," Frank said. "He either forgot or just didn't know." Frank's condition worsened and he was admitted to the hospital. "I remember Dr. Norment sitting there in my hospital room going through a medical book trying to figure out what to do."

Dorothy Frank ran out of patience as she watched her husband become deathly ill, despite his hospital treatment. She phoned her brother-in-law, Dr. Lou Goss, in Philadelphia and described her husband's worsening physical condition.

Dr. Goss ordered, by phone, 50,000 units of antitoxins immediately. Once the medication was administered, Frank had an adverse reaction. "The pain was excruciating," Frank said. "I got worse and became delirious. By midnight I was in an ambulance on the way to Duke Hospital."

At Duke, Frank was met by a Swedish, chain-smoking physician named Dr. Hanson-Pruss, but his situation continued to deteriorate. Frank was given a cup of water with a glass straw, which he promptly bit into and cracked because he couldn't control his jaw muscles. His mouth was filled with tiny shards of broken glass.

Hospital nurses pried open Frank's mouth and extracted the broken glass. He was injected with heavy doses of penicillin that Duke had obtained from the U.S.Army at Fort Bragg. Penicillin was not readily available for civilians in those war days. Frank never asked how Duke was able to get it from the Army.

"I was pretty cloudy for several days and don't remember too much," Frank said. "I just know I was in bad shape." It took physical therapy to restore use of his muscles. "I owe a lot to Dr. Hanson and to Dorothy's brother-in-law. They saved me when doctors in Greensboro could not, or did not."

While recovering from the immediate dangers of his lockjaw illness, Frank was ordered by Duke doctors to rest. He and Dorothy went to the Greystone Inn in Roaring Gap, North Carolina, for what was to be a week of relaxation so he could regain strength. The day after arriving at Greystone, he was called about a crisis at the rendering plant. He returned to Greensboro, ending his recuperation after one day.

Two years later, in 1946, Frank was back at Wesley Long Hospital for an appendectomy. That seemingly routine surgery also turned out badly.

Several months after his appendix was removed by Dr. Russell Lyday, Frank became seriously ill and wound up in Duke Hospital a second time. He continued to worsen and Duke doctors were unable to determine the cause. Once more, Dorothy Frank turned to her sister's physician husband in Pennsylvania for

help. In severe pain, Frank and his wife flew to Philadelphia to be treated by Dr. Goss. Goss and an associate performed a second surgery and discovered that
Dr. Lyday had failed to properly tie off Frank's intes-
tines. Frank was suffering internal poisoning from a
leakage from the prior surgery. The doctors removed
a section of his diseased lower intestine to correct the
problem.

"I would say that Dorothy's brother-in-law, Lou
Goss, saved my life twice," Frank said in the spring of
2000. "I'm fortunate to be alive, I guess, but Lou is
due a lot of the credit. He's the reason I'm still here."

Frank survived those two close calls in the 1940s
just as he did later surgery to remove potentially malignant polyps in the early 1980s. A more recent health
issue was still being monitored in the spring of 2001.
During a routine annual physical examination in 1998
at the Greenbrier Clinic, doctors discovered a dark spot
on Frank's lung.

A former cigarette smoker, Frank quit that habit
40 years before the spot was found. Doctors at the
Greenbrier suggested further tests. Frank went to Bowman Gray Medical Center in Winston-Salem, where he
has been involved as a financial contributor for many
years. A doctor there suggested an operation to excise
the spot, even as he abruptly added a troubling ca-
veat. "You may not survive the surgery," Frank recalled the doctor saying matter-of-factly. "I was sitting there with Dorothy when he said I might not survive. Well, that got our attention. We decided to get
another opinion."

Subsequent examination and monitoring of the
lung problem at Johns Hopkins Hospital determined
that surgery was not needed.

Frank's bad experiences with Greensboro doctors and hospitals in the 1940s were one reason in the early 1980s he accepted a seat on the board of a new hospital, Humana, which opened in Greensboro as competition for Wesley Long and Moses Cone.

He encountered a lot of criticism for joining up with out-of-state Humana, a for-profit hospital, both from his friends with ties to the two existing hospitals and from the local newspaper that was critical of Humana's pricing methods.

"Humana did what it was supposed to do," Frank said. "It opened up medical treatment in this community. I was criticized because they were making a profit. But what were Cone and Wesley Long doing? They were making money, just not paying taxes."

Humana lasted for a while, but the competition was too great from the already established hospitals. Cone Hospital later absorbed Humana. By the end of the 1990s, Cone and Wesley Long merged to form one huge medical complex, effectively eliminating all local hospital competition. "They are doing a good job with their foundations to help the community," Frank said of the hospital mergers, "but I have always felt that the American system was based on competition."

•

World War II brought Frank two other experiences, one connected with the war effort and one with helping people with personal problems in Greensboro.

During World War II, Frank served as a member of a little-known, yet important, part of the defense effort called the Fat Salvage Committee, a government-backed group designed to promote the manufacture of nitroglycerin.

Carolina By-Products was the only real rendering plant in North Carolina in the early 1940s, making Frank's role with the plant even more important to the government for its glycerin supply. As a member of the fat salvage effort, he encouraged housewives to save bacon drippings and other leftover grease from home cooking to use in the manufacture of soap and thus increased production of fat for glycerin.

Women who provided grease drippings were awarded points during war product rationing to be used to purchase other household goods that were also in short supply.

"What the government was doing at the time as part of the war effort was really amazing," Frank said. "It was inconceivable that they could set up the rationing boards and make them work. I think the success of many domestic war efforts came out of experiences from the Depression when people learned to be ingenious. The Depression in that regard was a great educator."

After the end of the war, Frank served on what was known as the Job Contact Committee, a local program designed to help rehabilitate alcoholics and get them into the job market to alleviate the labor shortage.

Frank said there was limited success in that effort, primarily because while the committee members were well intended, they didn't have specific skills in helping people stop drinking. "There were no great successes, but we did help some people," he said.

Those are the kinds of local projects, however, that helped convince Frank that more ought to be done to help fill needs in the local community and he was determined to become an active partner in filling that void.

As he continued to build his business, particularly after he purchased the company in 1953, he also steadily expanded his influence in helping lead a series of community endeavors that earned him deserved recognition as a person of seemingly unbounded energy who could get things done.

Frank's community achievements have been wide spread because rather than concentrate on a few projects, he scattered his interests and involvement. His depth has not been as great as some other Greensboro area philanthropists' have, but his breadth has been much wider than most.

Two of his most significant and long-time interests have been the regional airport and Guilford College. His imprint is solidly on both.

7

Cooperative Benevolence

World War II ended Sept. 2, 1945, less than a month after President Harry Truman, with the support of United States allies, directed the dropping of atomic bombs on Hiroshima and Nagasaki, Japan.

The euphoria was pronounced all across the country as the soldiers began returning home and the swell of patriotism flowed freely through homes, businesses and boardrooms. A grateful nation opened its arms to the returning war heroes who resumed their earlier lives in factories and on farms.

Thanks to a generous Congress, the GI Bill of Rights provided resources for thousands of returning veterans to enroll in colleges and universities for training or retraining and helped finance loans for homes, farms and businesses for thousands more. With the homecoming, however, came adjustments in how businesses were to be run and changes in the people who would run them.

Peacetime production was, quite often, significantly different from wartime manufacturing. This was certainly the situation with the rendering business at Carolina By-Products where there was an immediate need to shift emphasis on certain of its products and find alternate ways of turning out material that new, non-defense markets would embrace.

Stanley Frank, of course, was among those cheering the war's end. It stopped the killing, reunited families, provided the company he managed with a needed supply of workers and opened up access for essential supplies that had been hard to acquire during the tumultuous war years. Gasoline, tires and parts for company vehicles and other equipment had been scarce because of government-imposed restrictions while battles raged in Europe and Asia. Because of the military's critical need for glycerin, Frank had less difficulty than many company managers did in purchasing such needed supplies to keep businesses running during the war, though he had to deal with rationing just as everyone else did.

The war's end, however, brought an end to the high demand for glycerin from the soap manufacturing processes at Carolina By-Products. As a result, Frank began searching for new ways to achieve the best use of products from animal fats. He needed more expertise on chemical compounds and components to create the right products for changing markets. Neither Frank nor his employees at the time had the chemical knowledge required to develop these new products.

Frank turned to an expert. He asked Dr. Charles Ott, head of the chemistry department at Guilford College, for guidance. Little did either man know at the time what dividends that request and subsequent assistance would pay for so long.

"We were just looking for ways to find new uses for surplus animal fats after the war," Frank said of his first meeting with Dr. Ott shortly after World War II. "The high demand for glycerin no longer existed. We needed to find new markets for fats and other products and to convert materials once used in glycerin production to other uses."

"I honestly can't recall details of the first thing the professor worked on," Frank said of Ott. "But I know he helped with our animal fat production problem, with the war over. He helped get us on the right track for future growth"

The result of that assistance — for Frank and Guilford College — has been phenomenal. From those early contacts with Dr. Ott, Carolina By-Products in the early 1960s created an entirely new chemical division that has turned out numerous products for both homes and the textile industry. While Frank owned and later managed the company's Greensboro operation for other owners, that division represented a sizable percentage of the company's business and through the years generated significant revenue and profits.

More significantly for the community and the college, that initial cooperation between Dr. Ott and Frank has resulted in considerable monetary contributions from Frank and his family to Guilford College, fostering more than 30 years of leadership and service from Frank for the Quaker institution.

All that service and all those donations started with the help from the chemistry professor. If Frank had not asked or if Ott had declined to help, none of the future financial and leadership assistance might have existed. "The college and Dr. Ott were very helpful to my company and me when I needed help," Frank said. "I wanted to return the favor. Our relationship has been mutually beneficial."

That is an understatement.

Frank and his family have donated significant dollars toward the cost of the state-of-the-art science and technology complex that opened in the fall of 2000 on the Guilford College campus. The science center, initially projected to cost $10.5 million but climbing to more than $15 million by the time it was completed, is named the Frank Family Science Center because of Frank's many years of service and generous gifts to the school.

The science facility, however, is only the latest in a series of Frank family contributions to the college. Frank in the early 1980s created the Dorothy and Stanley Frank Fellows program that provides academic scholarships for students interested in business careers and entrepreneurship. The Franks have contributed generously for those scholarships that, among other things, focus on leadership and entrepreneurial approaches to business.

The Franks' Sedgefield home, valued at more than three-fourths of a million dollars, will become the property of Guilford College at their deaths or if they relocate to another residence.

Frank became a trustee at Guilford in 1969 and has served continuously for 31 years. He served prior to that on the college's board of visitors, on which his two sons, Bill and Barry, and daughter- in-law Hughlene were continuing to serve into the 21st century.

Frank's trustee service has included time as acting chairman, chairman of the executive committee, and vice chairman of the board. College regulations require that trustees retire from the board at age 72, but exceptions are allowed for annual reappointment beyond that age if a member's value to the school is considered especially important. That system has allowed Frank to continue to serve as a trustee; he accepted one-year appointments for each of the past 14 years at the end of the 20th century. He is among the most senior trustees in length of service in the school's long history — certainly the positive result of that initial cooperation between Dr. Ott and Frank following World War II.

Guilford administrators list Frank and his wife Dorothy among the top five donors to the school, dating from its founding in 1837. (Others on that top contributor list are Charles Dana, Joe Bryan Jr., Ed and Vivien Bauman, and Curt and Pat Hege.)

Frank is also the first Jew to serve as a Guilford trustee. President Grimsley Hobbs, in the late 1960s, opened the school's trustee membership to non-Quakers. The first two outsiders were Seth Macon of Greensboro, a Baptist, and William Linwood Beamon of Burlington, a Methodist. Both are graduates of Guilford.

Hobbs also wanted to include a person of Jewish faith among trustees and sought advice and recommendations from Greensboro Jewish community leaders. Frank wasn't nearly as well known at the time as other Jews in Greensboro, but he was the unanimous choice among Jewish businessmen in Greensboro for the post. His leadership and continuing interest have proven his selection to be a wise one.

Frank has also given generously of his time and talents over several decades at both Wake Forest University and the University of North Carolina at Greensboro. He is considered by leaders of both universities important to their success and development.

Frank has also worked with North Carolina A&T State University in Greensboro on various projects, most directly in efforts to establish a World Trade Center on the campus with the school's faculty and students a part of the project.

"He was the person with foresight to know the need for the World Trade Center and to understand the importance of it to this community," said Susan Howard Schwartz, a former staff member of one of the civic organizations involved in the creation of the trade zone. "He arranged the financing, got it going and just kept working at it."

The World Trade Center was created locally to help boost export/import trade involving local industries. Frank, while serving as chairman of the Piedmont Triad Airport Authority, was instrumental initially in securing a franchise for the Center and then for helping merge the Triad Center with one in the Raleigh-Durham area, now known as the World Trade Center North Carolina. His particular interest in expanding international trade dates to his years of managing Carolina By-Products Company, where exports were a significant portion of the business. He wanted the same for other local industries.

"Unfortunately it has had only moderate success," Frank said with a degree of disappointment in his voice. "Larger industries here already had their own international trade system in place and we didn't have enough smaller companies with enough interest to get a lot accomplished."

Frank's plans for the Center included incorporating it into educational instruction at both the University of North Carolina at Greensboro and at A&T

University with the headquarters to be on the A&T campus. A&T professor Dr. William James credits Frank with having the vision to work to create the Center and for efforts to keep it active while he was airport authority chairman.

Frank is the recipient of an honorary degree from Wake Forest and was chosen for the University of North Carolina at Greensboro Hall of Fame for services to that campus. His affection for each university is apparent when he talks of his ties to the campuses. But Guilford holds a special spot in his heart because of the cooperation afforded by Dr. Ott when a specific need existed and also because of the open approach to learning and tolerance the school promotes.

Quakers founded Guilford in 1837. While the school is an independent, liberal arts institution, it still adheres to many of the Quaker traditions relating to human conditions and open acceptance of people with divergent views.

Frank understands and accepts that approach because of his own philosophy and tolerant Jewish faith. Religious discrimination has never been a major factor in Frank's life, but he has encountered subtle vestiges, including what was once a clear signal that he would not be accepted for membership at Sedgefield Country Club. Later, however, he was welcomed into that club.

"I've just always felt, as a Jew, as much at home in my association with Guilford as with any other organization," Frank volunteered. "I've always been impressed with the Quaker tolerance toward minorities, because I am one, and their belief in independent thinking. Religious undercurrents don't exist there. I've always felt a part of the organization and felt comfortable there. I've always felt I had an equal chance there and they've always listened to my ideas and suggestions. There has always been a closeness for me with Guilford. I've gotten an education myself from that association. It has been a good fit."

Frank's long time friend and fellow Guilford trustee Seth Macon supports Frank's own assessment of his fondness for the school. "He has always said to me that he feels right at home there because of the feeling of respect, " Macon commented. "He has said that sometimes he thinks some Quakers are more like Jews than some Jews. He likes the consensus way of reaching decisions."

That has not, however, meant that Frank has readily approved of all the school's decisions during his long tenure on the board. He has not. He expressed strong opposition to the decision a decade ago to sever investment ties with companies dealing with South Africa because of apartheid. "I thought that action was going too far and told them I thought it was a mistake," he said, "but they did it anyway. While I didn't agree with it, the decision was certainly the majority feeling among trustees so I accepted it."

"His contributions to Guilford have been significant in dollars and energy," in the words of the school's vice president for institutional advancement Charles Patterson, "but his service goes far beyond that. He has been able to open up all kinds of doors for us because of his many connections. He has done so much for so many people in this community and he willingly goes to those people to ask them to help us. He expects them to respond. There is not much good for this college or this city that he hasn't been involved in helping promote."

Frank's friend Macon agrees. "He has maintained connections everywhere. He is the best networking person I've ever known. He works those relationships and just keeps on working. I admire his tenacity. He is always thinking of ways to make things better for the college and the community."

Frank's devotion to Guilford was apparent to former college president William Rogers and current president Don McNemar the day each met him. Frank was involved in the selection of both and met with each before they were chosen. Both were impressed with his energy and his enthusiasm in their initial sessions with him.

"He has taught me a great deal about civic leadership," Rogers said. "He was an important part of my life at Guilford. He has been a major plus for Guilford and has shown how a person in the business world can also be a passionate contributor to public causes. He provides a real balance between the two. His interest in the free enterprise system has extended to academic programs. He became the bridge between the college and business and has stepped forward as a key advocate for entrepreneurial leadership and values.

"He has always had a passionate intensity to reach goals and an abiding faith in the American way of life. He has the dual capacity to work through disagreements honestly and still preserve friendships. He is what I would call a born leader and a loyal friend because he has always been available to help, always with a twinkle in his eye and a warm sense of humor toward getting things done in the right way."

When he was being interviewed for the presidency to replace the retiring Rogers on June 1, 1996,

McNemar met Frank at a private lunch in Greensboro. "He gave me a great sense of this community. He showed a tremendous sense of energy and had that constant twinkle about him even though he was direct in his approach. I quickly determined that he was committed to the Quaker approach to an open environment and was committed to change." Frank's candid approach was one reason McNemar accepted the job.

The two communicate regularly, seldom going more than a few days without talking. "He's always available, but he doesn't hesitate to tell you when he feels you're wrong. I'm certainly proud of his involvement with Guilford and think it is fully appropriate to have the new science facility with his name attached," McNemar said.

McNemar has also seen Frank's subtle sense of humor used as a way of reaching consensus on critical issues. During one serious discussion when he felt differing opinions were becoming a bit overheated, Frank provided a soothing peace offering. "That's OK," he said, "I'm a lover, not a fighter." It worked. The issue was resolved.

Frank started the Frank Fellows scholarship program in 1983 as one means of putting more emphasis on innovative ways of teaching students with interests in business. He provided scholarship aid, $1,500 a year at the time, for students meeting guidelines that included internships and mentoring with local business owners.

"His approach was different," said Art Gillis, former vice president at Guilford. "He wanted entrepreneurship, something students couldn't get from textbooks. His purpose was to teach students about business in the real sense."

The Fellows program drifted for a few years in the 1990s because of lack of structure and what appeared to Frank as mentoring with little meaning. Frank asked for revisions and that was done with the beginning of the 1998 academic year. Fellows are now limited to juniors and seniors, guidelines are stricter, written assessments on mentoring are required, research projects on entrepreneurship are mandatory to build a reservoir of library materials and sessions are regularly held with local entrepreneurs.

Scholarships have been increased to $2,000 a year with renewal each semester if recipients meet guidelines. One hundred and forty students have received scholarship aid since the program was started.

Frank created the Fellows program, he said, because he felt most college campuses offered little in the way of real business experience or training and because of the importance of risk-taking and entrepreneurship in his own career. "I wouldn't be where I am today without that approach to business," he said. "I've never felt the American system of free enterprise was taught very well, except maybe in theory. Most college professors know little about the way a system of business actually works. Some of them, in fact, are pretty much anti-business. Dorothy and I set up this program to help provide some balance and better understanding of business and entrepreneurial efforts among students."

Jonathan Bostock, a 1999 Guilford College graduate from Amhurst, Massachusetts, was one of the Frank Fellows during his senior year. "It was a wonderful opportunity to learn and be exposed to things that most students never get a chance to see or do during their college careers," Bostock said in assessing the program. "And Mr. Frank was genuinely interested in us. He cared and made us feel we were special."

In January 1998, Guilford trustees approved a plan to raise money for building a new science building on the campus. Frank, not suprisingly, was asked to be supportive and, not surprisingly, he agreed. "I had no idea at that time that anyone was going to propose that my name be put on the building," he said.

As plans for the new building progressed, however, discussions on choosing a name and Frank's long and continuous contributions came together. He agreed to the name, but only if it included his family, not just himself. The Frank Family Science Center opened in the fall of 2000 as a centerpiece of the campus.

Frank's contributions to the college through the years have clearly reached the millions, easily enough to justify, in the eyes of college administrators and his fellow trustees, the naming of the science building for his family. The total cost of the facility has surpassed $15 million, including an auditorium named for Joseph Bryan Jr., a longtime trustee, with a $1 million contribution from the foundation created by Bryan's father, Greensboro philanthropist Joseph McKinley Bryan Sr.

The 63,500 square foot, four-story building along New Garden Road was designed for learning through close partnerships between faculty and students. There are 14 laboratories with 24 workspaces each. The facility is wired with the most up to date electronic equipment, a rooftop observatory with a computer-driven telescope, a planetarium and a 166-seat auditorium. It replaces the former science building, built more than 30 years earlier.

Naming the science building for the Frank family is in keeping with the long tradition of choosing donor names for facilities on the campus: Hege Library, Dana Auditorium, Ragsdale House.

Sitting just a few yards from the Frank Family building is a relatively new classroom building named for retired Greensboro businessman Ed Bauman and his wife Vivien. Bauman and Frank have been long-time friends, as well as generous supporters of Guilford College; each has made contributions to the building named for the other. Bauman, an engineering graduate of Purdue University and former Blue Bell Corporation executive, shares Frank's penchant for entrepreneurial approaches to business. Bauman and his wife have donated $3.75 million to Guilford in recent years.

"He's a feisty little guy," Bauman said of his friend Frank. "He is dedicated, persistent and has worked hard behind the scenes for a long time. He deserves the recognition he is now receiving. He is as fine a person as there is anywhere."

•

Frank's involvement with the University of North Carolina at Greensboro has been closely tied to athletics and nursing. At Wake Forest, his initial interests lay with the school of arts and sciences and athletics, but he has also been supportive of research at the medical school, particularly cancer research.

When the Frank's second son Barry was a child

in the early 1950s, he was treated for epilepsy by physicians at the Bowman Gray Medical School, but that was the family's only connection with the Baptist university until the middle 1970s. The second connection came through the Greensboro Sports Council following a basketball game in the Greensboro Coliseum. His involvement as an active participant in medical research came later.

Frank, long a sports fan as well as one of the founding partners of the original Greensboro Generals professional hockey team, made known his interest in the Wake Forest Deacons during a reception after a Wake Forest game with another Atlantic Coast Conference team at the Greensboro Coliseum.

"I have a perfectly pleasant memory of how it came about," said Frank's friend Charles Reid, a Greensboro mortgage company official and Wake Forest graduate. "He and I were both at a reception in the (coliseum) Blue Room following a game. Stanley just walked up to me and started the conversation."

"Charlie, I never got an education here and have never had any connection with any big four (Wake Forest, the University of North Carolina, North Carolina State, Duke University) school," Frank said. "But I like Wake Forest. I like the team and I'd be interested in getting involved."

"Well, that's the only push I needed," Reid said. "Present at the reception were then Wake president Ralph Scales, athletics director Gene Hooks and basketball coach Carl Tacy. I introduced Stanley to each of them, and each was genuinely receptive to getting him involved. That's how it all started, after the basketball game. But it was Stanley who took the initiative."

Shortly after that meeting to talk sports, Greensboro businessman Al Lineberry Sr., also a strong Wake supporter, took Frank to the Wake Forest campus for the first time and introduced him again to President Scales and other administrators. Lineberry suggested that Frank be named to the campus Board of Visitors. At the time, Jews were not permitted to serve on the board of trustees.

Frank soon developed a warm friendship with Scales that lasted until Scales' death in 1996. In May 1981, Scales showed his appreciation for Frank's service and contribution to the university by awarding him an honorary Doctor of Humanities degree.

"Stanley has never been interested in just having his name on a roster," Reid said. "He wants to be involved, to make things happen. When he decides something ought to be done, it can't be done fast enough. He is a person of action. If you don't like his ideas, you'd better tell him. If you don't, he'll expect you to get it done. He can always get things accomplished. He has always been a positive influence on his community with the things he has done or caused to be done. If he sees a problem, he wants it solved before the sun goes down. I've learned a lot from him."

In addition to his involvement with Wake Forest, Reid has worked closely with Frank through First Union National Bank where Reid was once an officer and Frank was on the board of directors, both locally and corporately.

"President Scales asked me for names of people who might be able to help Wake Forest, and I gave him Stanley's name," Lineberry said. "I knew Stanley liked to be involved in things with substance. President Scales and the people at Wake Forest paid attention to his ideas. He appreciated that and I think Wake gave him the kind of university association that he was never able to have as a young man. His involvement with Wake Forest has kept him and the school moving forward."

"I always felt that maybe Al (Lineberry) was courting me on behalf of Wake Forest because he was looking for someone who could make financial contributions," Frank said. "But there is nothing wrong with that. I was willing to help. I've been a supporter of the school in time and money because I felt it was a worthy endeavor."

It was not until after Frank's service on the Board of Visitors that Wake Forest amended its trustee guidelines to allow Jewish members. "If the rule had been changed earlier as it should have been, Stanley would have been the first Jew named because he deserved that honor," Lineberry said. "He has always stayed busy helping others wherever there was a need." When Lineberry was seeking funds for the Association of Baptists for Scouting, Frank made the first $1,000 contribution.

"Wake Forest is a classy organization, but entirely different from Guilford College," Frank said of his involvement with the two schools. "Neither is superior in any way to the other. But they are just two different institutions with different purposes. (President) Tom Hearn has given Wake a big boost in stature. It's a darn fine university and I'm glad to be associated with it. And I always admired Ralph Scales, who was a close friend, a fine leader and just a good country gentleman. He was the first to move the school away from the close association with the Baptist Church, which was a good move."

Scales became president of Wake Forest in 1967, almost a decade after Wake Forest relocated from the town of the same name in Wake County to Winston-Salem. Scales and Frank were a lot alike in personality, both relatively quiet and with little flamboyancy. But both were also men of action. That's perhaps why they worked so well together. Part American Indian from Oklahoma, Scales was a relative of Will Rogers.

Scales also helped to promote Frank's interest in medical research at Wake Forest, an effort that has paid off in financial dividends and leadership service on the board and steering committee of the Wake Forest Comprehensive Cancer Center.

"We are indebted to him for several reasons," said Dr. Frank Torti, director of the Wake cancer research unit. "He has given money for research, but his thoughtfulness and understanding of needs have been equally important. His efforts have helped us do more with gene therapy and with embryo therapy. What sets him apart is his attention to detail and his wonderful perception. He follows through on everything. He leaves nothing open and if he promises something, it will be done. His financial contributions, while not as large as some others, have been used as leverage and he gives in such a way to gain maximum use of his resources. He has been a real leader of the lay membership on our board. I admire him greatly for what all he has done to help us here. He sees a need and strives to fill it."

Dr. Richard Janeway, Wake Forest's executive vice president for Health Affairs emeritus, echoes those same sentiments. "I've never met a person with as much energy for so many worthwhile projects," said Dr. Janeway, who retired in June 1997 and is now university professor of medicine and management. "He bellies up to the bar and takes initiatives that others lack. People serve on boards because they possess wit, wisdom or wealth. Stanley posses all three. He is the epitome of those people who are willing to pick up meaningful things to help others."

Dr. Janeway cited one example. "We were in need of some training funds. At a board meeting, Stanley volunteered to provide what we needed. He said 'I'll do that' and he did. By his actions, he makes more people cognizant of needs. He leads and others follow. He is one of our biggest boosters and he has helped get others involved. He has been a valuable member of our board."

Dr. Janeway's wife, Katherine (Kathy), who has worked with Frank on the cancer center board, offered her own assessment. "He's a wonderful cheerleader for what we are doing at the center," she said. "He is fully committed to worthy projects and inspires others. He is always asking why we're not doing this or doing that. His interest and energy are bountiful."

•

"Stanley doesn't make a lot of waves with what he does; he is a doer, not a talker."

That is the assessment of the University of North Carolina at Greensboro Chancellor Pat Sullivan and Athletics Director Nelson Bobb. "He's the kind of person you can bounce ideas off and get candid responses," Bobb said. "He's a tough businessman who can be firm, but one with vision who is always fair. His advice and wisdom have been valuable to this university and he's a man I can call on as a son would call on a father. His generosity personally and professionally is outstanding."

Chancellor Sullivan calls Frank one of the most valuable University of North Carolina at Greensboro supporters for his private advice as well as public support. "He's a very astute businessman who can zero in on issues and find solutions," she said. "But I also value him for his private counsel and advice. He is a dedicated supporter of the university, but also a very warm and caring person."

Frank is one of the "Big Five" among the University of North Carolina at Greensboro Excellence Fund donors with athletic scholarship contributions of more than $10,000 each. Those five — Frank, Charles (Chuck) Hayes, Jim Melvin, Charlie Reid, and Mike Weaver — were chosen for their contributions as part of the University of North Carolina at Greensboro's successful move to Division I category in NCAA competition. The five, who have helped raise more than $2.3 million for athletic scholarships, were inducted into the University of North Carolina at Greensboro Hall of Fame on September 29, 2000.

A plaque in Frank's honor was erected at the campus baseball stadium. After being asked to throw out the first ball on the day the new baseball stadium opened, Frank held several private practice sessions to keep his arm loose for the day of the official pitch.

Frank has served as a member of the University of North Carolina at Greensboro Excellence Fund committee, the Board of Visitors, and the university's Nursing Advisory Board since its formation in 1987, serving as chairman since 1989. "I guess I'm sort of their permanent board chairman," he said with a chuckle. "The chancellor says it is okay for me to keep the job. I'm happy to do it. It is certainly a wonderful school."

"His contributions are many, but there is absolutely no ego involved," Sullivan said of Frank's efforts on behalf of the local university campus. "He gets things done quietly and with dedication."

8

Flying Early & Often

Stanley Frank vividly recalled those two special days in the spring of 1927, remembering intimate details almost three-fourths of a century later, notwithstanding the fact that he was a skinny lad not yet 13 at the time.

Those were the two days in May when his hero, Charles Augustus Lindbergh, did what no man had ever done, and what some naysayers predicted no man would ever do. Lindbergh flew solo nonstop in a single engine airplane, the *Spirit of St. Louis*, from New York to Paris, flying 3,610 miles in 33.5 hours. A trip that began in the early morning hours of New York on May 20 ended in the late hours of May 21 in Paris.

"It was a fascinating thing for me. Lindbergh was definitely one of my early heroes," Frank readily acknowledged. "I had been intrigued with airplanes, even before his flight. I remember seeing some early homemade planes at aviation shows in New York's Hippodrome, near my home. I have been fascinated with flying ever since. But it was Lindbergh's flight that made it all more real. He was a great stimulus for me."

Frank's first public display of his love for flying actually came as a ten-year-old grammar student. When asked in literature class to write on any preferred topic, he penned a poem about an airplane. He remembered his exact words more than 75 years later:

A whir, a whine, and then a light.

And out of the upheaval dark of night
an airplane came into my sight.

It was a mighty monarch of the air.
Birdlike, but not quite as fair.

The historic transatlantic flight was an amazing accomplishment for Lindbergh and the fledgling flying industry in the United States, even though money was the primary incentive. Lindbergh wanted to succeed for the sake of enhancing the progress of flying, to be sure, but his prime motivation was to collect the $25,000 prize money offered eight years earlier by New York hotel owner Raymond Orteig to the first pilot to make the nonstop trip.

For young Frank, this Staten Island teenager, his affection for flying became an obsession as Lindbergh made his way across the Atlantic before landing at Le Bourget Field in Paris.

Lindbergh wasn't the first person to fly across at least part of the Atlantic, but he was the first to fly so far for so long without stopping, thus granting him the Lucky Lindy nickname and the most public recognition at that time as well as later in history books.

In 1919, eight years before Lindbergh's historic flight, two adventurous British pilots, John Alcock and

Arthur Whitten-Brown, flew from St. John's, Newfoundland, to Clifden, Ireland, a distance of 1,890 miles, roughly half the distance of Lindbergh's trip. Later, in the same year as Lindbergh's inaugural flight, Clarence Chamberlin was the first person to surpass the Lindbergh distance; Chamberlin flew more than 3,900 miles from New York to Eisleben, Germany, with one passenger on board.

Frank still talks with glee and animation when he discusses his recollections and readings about each of those early flights that made aviation history, even to naming the models of the planes. Lindbergh flew in a Ryan M-2 monoplane. Chamberlin made his flight in a Bellanca, a high-wing monoplane named for its Italian designer, Giuseppa Bellanca, a member of a family that designed a series of planes in the early part of the 20th century.

(Frank's Sedgefield home also had a brief brush with aviation history, albeit an indirect one, which he still takes pride in discussing. Amelia Earhart was an overnight guest in the home shortly before her own transatlantic solo flight in 1932. Frank purchased the home 18 years later.)

Frank didn't go outside during the almost 34 hours of his hero Lindbergh's successful flight. Instead, he hunkered down by the scratchy-sounding radio at his mother's Staten Island residence, listening to every news flash update of the famous flight. The next day, he spent more time sprawled on his belly on the parlor floor devouring the stories in *The New York Times*. He used the parlor for the experience, he said, because that room was reserved for special occasions. In young Frank's mind, his hero Lindbergh's flight was about as special as anything could get. It was, he thought, a dream come true for his new American hero.

He had a personal dream of flying that he wanted to turn into reality at the first opportunity.

He did, too, and Greensboro and the Piedmont Triad have been major beneficiaries. Frank brought his love of flying with him to Greensboro in 1936, when he arrived with little more than loose change in his pocket and the clothes on his back, and has been building on that love ever since.

People in the Piedmont Triad affectionately call him "Mr. Airport" for good reason. He was one of the city's earliest private pilots. Frank once told a magazine reporter that flying to him was like a good cry to a woman. "It cleanses the soul," he said. He has been a part of Greensboro's flying history and development for more than 60 years, serving as a member of the local airport authority for almost three decades and as its chairman for 20 years. He even served for a while — without pay — as the airport's chief executive and operations manager.

As airport authority chairman, he gave more service and energy to the airport over a longer period of time than any other individual. He also led the way for various other endeavors. Spearheading efforts, he

• secured land and planned for future airport expansion.

• was vitally connected to planning and construction, from start to finish. He made flights across the United States and parts of Europe, searching for the best ideas before the new passenger terminal was built in the early 1980s. He led the pursuit of the new terminal, perhaps his single greatest airport achievement.

• found the best deal on bonds to pay for the terminal, using his business skills and corporate connections to secure an interest rate that saved the airport authority millions of dollars in finance charges.

• secured aircraft maintenance facilities at the airport that has provided thousands of jobs and millions of dollars in economic growth for the region.

• established an airline industry educational and training facility that has a reputation as one of the best in the country.

• worked early on for economic regionalism with the airport as a cornerstone.

• urged preservation of land around the airport for air traffic rather than residential development, a point he lost even though history has proved he was right and many in the community later wished he had succeeded.

• extolled the merits of increased airfreight when few believed it would become such a huge part of the airline industry.

• helped pick the airport's present name as one means of bringing the region closer together, reducing the inter-city squabbling over which place had priority.

In a sense, Frank for decades made the local airport and its development his own mini-universe.

He tended to discount the personal credit he has received from Triad leaders for his influence over the decades at the airport, insisting that it was a team effort and credit ought to be spread to others as well. But the facts speak for themselves: Stanley Frank was directly responsible for a large part of what exists at the airport today. Few people anywhere have ever pursued their passion for total community enhancement with as much zeal and enthusiasm over a lifetime as Frank has. That assessment would certainly apply to his interest in the local airport and its development.

"The airport has been his mantra and is a testimony to his efforts," commented Tom Bradshaw, former head of the N. C. Department of Transportation. Bradshaw, an investment banker, managed the sale of bonds for the new terminal through what was then First Boston Corporation. "Stanley Frank has taken to that airport like it was one of his children."

"The airport is clearly what it is because of him," said Hudnall Christopher, current airport authority chairman and retired R. J. Reynolds executive. "He has been obsessed with making it the best. No one has ever been more dedicated to that effort, and he has laid a foundation for others to follow."

"Stanley truly loves that airport and what it has meant to the community," commented retired brick company executive Bill Jones, an airport authority member when Frank was chairman. "It has meant as much to him as his own business. He knew of its value to this community. No one has wanted the airport to succeed as much as he did."

"I have never known a more dedicated airport chairman," said William Howard, former president of Piedmont Airlines. "The Greensboro community could not have had a better chairman or finer person in that job. The community would not have the airport facility it has except for his efforts. He was dogged in his determination to see it succeed in spite of many difficulties."

"Without Stanley Frank's hard work and dedication, we quite likely would never have located at the airport," explained former Triad International Maintenance Corporation (TIMCO) executive Charles

Bell. "He made it happen with the foresight and determination to see it through." TIMCO pumps some $40 million a year into the region's economy.

"He is the one who got TIMCO here," former airport director of operations Floyd McKenzie said of Frank. "It hit a lot of snags in the process, but he wouldn't give up. He kept the effort going. That is just one of the many positive results of his efforts. Stanley Frank is a very astute businessman, a real dynamo who is hard to keep up with in his efforts and vision for this facility."

"He has always understood what a top-notch airport can mean for the people and the economy of this community," said airport executive director Ted Johnson. "He has consistently been passionate about making it first class. He has always been very good at negotiating with airlines for the benefit of the airport and customers. He was determined, tough when he needed to be, and had the political foundation to get things done. It took good leadership to achieve what he has accomplished. Stanley had both the vision and the power to succeed."

"He knew who to call and how to get things done," said American Airlines Piedmont Triad station manager Dennis Peterson. "He has been very helpful to commercial carriers, dedicated to excellence, and he made people want to excel. He was always asking what more he could do to make things better. Without him on the airport board, this community misses his wisdom, energy, communication skills and service."

Even former airport executive director Roger Sekadlo, who was never personally close to Frank because of personality clashes, offered praise. "He paid attention to needs and listened," Sekadlo said. "He helped put that master plan together and was proud of it. The new terminal came out of that. He pushed hard for it, more so than most board members did. He was a 'go-ahead-and-get-things-done' man of action."

"We would not have our teaching facility at the airport without him" Guilford Technical Community College President Don Cameron said of Frank. "He took the initiative and found the resources. No one has taken the airport more seriously than Stanley and no one has taken to heart more seriously the quality of life in this region."

Even so, however, the skies have often been choppy and the flights of success have not always been smooth. Quite the contrary. Political gamesmanship and determined doomsayers have hovered like a thick, dark winter storm over growth and planned airport development almost since the first flight landed. The battle lines were still being stretched across the tarmacs as the 21st century began, more than 70 years after the airport became a reality.

First, there were those who didn't want an airport when it was created in the late 1920s, a decade before Frank arrived in town. Then there were those who wanted the facility to be located in Winston-Salem, rather than where it is now, between Greensboro and Winston-Salem. Municipal jealousies have existed from the first airport discussions. Frank has worked for decades to defuse those feelings, focusing on the entire region rather than one city or the other.

Despite Frank's arguments against it, developers in the 1960s began building houses in flight patterns, on the cusp of airport runways. That battle was still raging into the year 2001 with the controversy over a proposed multi-million dollar Federal Express distribution center, a center that would boost the region's economy even as it disrupts some of the residential neighborhoods that Frank had wisely but unsuccessfully urged not be built.

Political meddling into airport authority membership in the 1990s cost the board decades of experience and knowledge when Frank was denied another term on the airport authority.

Furthermore, demographics have been a drawback to airport progress. Greensboro and the Piedmont region have not had state government or the Research Triangle Park as Raleigh does to help its airport growth. Greensboro has never had major financial centers as Charlotte does. Both Raleigh and Charlotte had an abundance of white-collar travelers while Greensboro was dealt a hand of textile and tobacco industries where the economic foundation and growth have not been as pronounced.

"Compared to those two areas, I guess maybe we didn't have a lot to sell," Frank said as he discussed airport growth, his dreams, and his preferences. "Most of our business travelers were those associated with blue collar industries. The volume of passengers and economic growth just have not been here."

Discounting his own achievements, in spite of evidence to the contrary, and questioning his own effectiveness, Frank outlined how some decisions might have made a difference.

"Maybe I wasn't as effective as I should have been in landing the American Airlines hub that went to Raleigh-Durham. I wish the authority could have convinced Southwest Airlines to come here years ago, but I hope they still will. I made some mistakes, but I worked the political situation the best I could. I had a good relationship with the heads of the FAA and CAB. We simply didn't have a whole lot to sell, compared to Charlotte and Raleigh. At times progress has seemed overly slow, but you don't turn the Queen Mary around without a lot of effort. We had the political situation that we didn't need and didn't have some growing industries that we did need."

When Frank began watching planes land there shortly after he arrived in town in January 1936, the local airport, then known as Lindley Field, was little more than a bumpy, grassy animal pasture with a small mound to help vintage planes swoop down for easier takeoffs or roll up as an aid for slowing landings. It was to him a place of pleasure as well as an economic stimulus and he made frequent visits, taking his first plane ride there in the spring of 1936 in an open cockpit biplane.

He began private flying lessons in 1956, thinking he was keeping a secret from his wife Dorothy, who he felt would not support his plans of piloting his own plane. He didn't tell her for months of his weekend lessons, but she knew. "I was just waiting for him to tell me, and he eventually did," she said. "He thought he was getting something past me, but I realized what he was doing." She wasn't initially thrilled with the idea, but later accepted his flying as a good idea for his business. Since then she has often flown with him as pilot in his own airplanes.

He purchased his first company plane in 1957, a Beech Bonanza, at a cost of $25,000. Four decades later, that same plane was selling for ten times that amount. He later purchased three other newer model company planes that he used for years in his business to reduce travel time among his many rendering plants. "I was running myself ragged, driving so much

Stanley and Dorothy Frank on March 5, 1989,
the date of their GoldenWedding Anniversary.

Stanley and Dorothy Frank with sons Bill (left) and Barry in March 1989.

The Frank family, March 1989, at Stanley and Dorothy's 50th Anniversary reception at Greensboro Country Club. Standing behind the couple is son Barry, his wife Carol, stepdaughters Katie and Kelly, daughter-in-law Hughlene and son Bill.

Stanley and Dorothy Frank (center) in April 1986 at a Wake Forest Medical School reception with friends John and Polly Medlin (left) and Tom Davis, President of Piedmont Airlines.

Stanley Frank (right center) with Vice President George Bush in Bush's White House office in 1981. Frank was one of three rendering plant executives from the United States meeting with the vice president to discuss government environmental regulations and more efficient use of animal by-products.

The English Tudor Frank family home facing Sedgefield Country Club golf course. Stanley and Dorothy Frank have donated the home to Guilford College.

Stanley Frank (second from left) with his partners following a charity golf tournament in the spring of 1998. With Frank are UNCG golf pro Ellen Lapierre, Marge Burns and Mike Burke.

The Frank Family Science Center at Guilford College. Stanley and Dorothy Frank gave substantial sums to help pay for the $15 million-plus facility. College officials chose to honor the Franks by naming the modern building for them. The auditorium is at the left and the observatory is at the upper right.

to the different plant sites," Frank said in explaining his need for planes to reduce his time on the highways of the state and region. But it was also a genuine pleasure for him each time he soared through the clouds. He also used the aircraft — always without charge — for countless flights that had far more to do with community betterment and civic work than his business bottom line.

Frank also allowed his company planes to be used for humanitarian purposes and was once credited with helping save the life of a young Raleigh Republican campaign worker. In 1972, shortly after James Holshouser was elected the first Republican governor in a century in North Carolina, a group of his campaign workers traveled to the Bahamas for a victory celebration. Their celebration went a bit too far and the revelers crashed their motorized island vehicle, which erupted in flames, severely burning Holshouser aide Bill Russell.

At the request of Holshouser's office, Frank provided his plane to fly to the Bahamas, pick up the burn victim and transport him to Duke Hospital. The governor's staff assistant Gene Anderson later wrote Frank a letter of appreciation, saying "I am convinced that Bill would have died in the Bahamian hospital if it had not been for your act of generosity because there was no other way for us to have gotten him home."

Anderson later said he remembered Frank was a Richard Nixon supporter with an airplane — although not a Holshouser supporter in the governor's campaign — and sought his help in getting the burn victim home. "He was most gracious and immediately offered his assistance," Anderson said. "Doctors at Duke told the burn victim he would have died in another day or two in the Bahamian hospital where sanitation standards were awful if Mr. Frank had not brought him back to North Carolina. Both Bill and I feel a deep appreciation to Mr. Frank for his life-saving intervention"

•

Greensboro's airport has had an important and lasting role in the history and development of the region, despite the many pitfalls and political infighting lasting almost three-fourths of a century. For the last half of the 20th century, Frank was a cornerstone, as the earlier testimony of business and airport associates attests.

While Charlotte and Raleigh-Durham airports have surpassed the local airport in recent decades in size and passenger volumes, what is now Piedmont Triad International Airport was once much further advanced and on the cutting edge of east coast air service.

Greensboro was the only stop in North Carolina

The airplane used in the inaugural airmail stop in Greensboro on May 1, 1928, at what was then Lindley Field. The plane, called the Mailwing, was owned by Pitcairn Aviation, a forerunner to Eastern Airlines. Greensboro was the first airmail stop in North Carolina. The inaugural flight drew more than 3,000 spectators.

for the original airmail route between New York and Atlanta. The maiden airmail flight for the state was recorded in the spring of 1927, an event of major proportions for the area as well as the state. The local airstrip was chosen by Pitcairn Aviation, a forerunner of Eastern Airlines, as the state's only airmail stop because of what was described as the quality of the runway, rudimentary though it was with grass and hillsides where cattle once grazed.

The landing strip in those early days was not far from where current runways are located. Originally, the airport was called Lindley Field at the community of Friendship because the airstrip was on land owned by Paul Lindley, a future city mayor who used part of the farmland property for his plant nursery.

Greensboro was chosen by Pitcairn after two years of lobbying by local leaders who wanted to ensure the local community was on the airmail route and after several test runs by the fledgling airline that had won a government contract to deliver mail to major cities via air. The local effort had been helped in the fall of 1926 when famed racing pilot Capt. Roscoe Turner set his plane down in the Lindley pasture and promptly declared the site the best landing field in the South. Turner especially liked the hill where pilots could roll up to slow their planes, some not equipped with brakes. And, if the wind was right, pilots could use the incline as an aid in takeoffs.

While there was strong sentiment among leaders in the region for airmail service in the middle and late 1920s, there was not easy agreement on where the airfield ought to be, or even if it ought to be. Already, municipal bickering and political differences were beginning to surface.

The region was then known as the "Triangle Cities" (Greensboro, High Point and Winston-Salem), and leaders in each city wanted a bigger piece of the airport pie than they felt leaders in the other two places were willing to give. That was the beginning of turf wars among the cities.

An airstrip site was sought as close as equidistant from the three towns as possible. After months of wrangling and several rejections by one town or the other, a tentative site that initially seemed to satisfy all three was found, bordering the Guilford-Forsyth county lines near Kernersville. But it was not cheap.

Some local leaders from each of the three towns, while supporting the concept of airmail service, objected to spending much money on something as untested as air travel and, furthermore, something as uncertain as airmail delivery. There were those who, no pun intended, said air service would never fly and that money should not be wasted on such risky ventures. That displeasure toward engaging in unproven economic ventures has lingered in the Triad since those early days, and not just at the airport — although that's where it began.

Paul Lindley, playing the role as peacemaker, offered his property closer to Greensboro as an alternative airstrip site if no agreement could be reached on other locations. Lindley reminded local officials that barnstorming pilots, after all, had used his land often without any problems and no less than famed daredevil pilot Turner had blessed it as safe and convenient.

Lindley proposed a deal: he would lease his 113 acres to an airport commission or local government entity at no direct cost for up to ten years in exchange for exemption from his property taxes. (Lindley at the time was privately suffering some economic difficulties and the tax exemption was a financial benefit to him.) He also offered local officials an option to buy his land at what he called a "reasonable price" at any time during the lease.

When James Ray, operations manager for Pitcairn, landed his plane during his test run on the Lindley property as local business leaders watched, he figuratively rolled right into Lindley's lap. That strip was just fine for airmail traffic, Ray declared, and the county line site he later toured offered nothing positive as an alternative. The Lindley site, Ray stressed, could be made ready in a few hours with a couple of mules and a harrow while the county line location would take much more work and be no better. That sealed the deal.

Or so it was thought. While the site selection

One of the earliest passenger planes to use the Greensboro airport in the early 1930s. The plane was used for airmail and passenger service and was operated by what was then Eastern Air Transport. The first passenger flight out of Greensboro was December 10, 1930.

committee from the three towns lost their enthusiasm for the county line and agreed to the Lindley offer of land use in lieu of tax payments, their agreement lasted only six months.

The cities decided to purchase the Lindley land. In September 1927 when Greensboro and High Point put money ($16,500 and $5,000 respectively) with their verbal promise to purchase the Lindley property, Winston-Salem backed out.

The Lindley land was ten miles from the city limits of Greensboro and High Point, but 20 miles from Winston-Salem. The Winston leaders said that was just too far away and they decided to take a different flight toward air service. Greensboro and High Point proceeded without Winston's support.

The Reynolds Foundation in Winston-Salem then put up cash to open what became Smith Reynolds Airport, and Winston-Salem went its own way. History would eventually prove, of course, that it made no economic sense to have two commercial airports so close together, but the inter-city distrust continued unabated for decades and, in fact, has never completely gone away.

"Unfortunately, that competition has been going on among the cities since the 1920s and early 1930s," Frank explained in discussing the region's air service history. "Each city wanted more. Tom Davis was the founder and then president of Piedmont Airlines, which at the time was based in Winston-Salem. Davis had a lot of pressure on him from the business people of Winston to keep passenger service there. It was tough, but he was always fair with us in Greensboro. Bill Howard, Davis' successor, actually cut the final Piedmont passenger service at Smith Reynolds

Airport. Most of that business came to the regional airport. That was a happy day for this airport and me. We had the better facilities. Though the change made sense, it was no easy decision. Bill Howard deserves the credit for having the courage to do that."

At one time, with both airports seeking and obtaining service, the competition between Eastern and Piedmont airlines was stiff. Routinely, one or both commercial airlines would make passenger stops at both airports. Quickly realizing such a schedule was losing money, Eastern pulled out from Smith Reynolds, followed by Piedmont at the direction of Howard.

Frank directs much of the credit for the growth and development of the regional airport to Davis, despite economic pressures on Davis to divert more attention to the Winston-Salem airport. "He was my mentor and advisor for much of what we have achieved at the regional airport," Frank said. "He deserves the credit. He was always cooperative, helpful and a great source of ideas."

Frank and Davis maintained a close personal and professional relationship over several decades. Davis died April 22, 1999, at age 81. The GTCC aviation-training center at the airport bears Davis' name. He gave $250,000 to keep the program viable and growing because his friend Frank made the request. Frank was one of the people involved in pushing for more growth on the GTCC instructional facility and first proposed that it be named in honor of Davis. Davis asked that the building be named for Frank, but Frank declined, saying Davis was the deserving choice.

Despite Winston-Salem's reneging on the promise to help purchase the Lindley land, Greensboro and High Point pooled their resources to buy the property that became the airmail drop prior to any passenger service being started.

Pitcairn, which manufactured its own airplanes designed especially for mail delivery and dubbed them "mailwings," began regular airmail service at the local airport on the night of May 1, 1928.

The inaugural airmail stop in Greensboro was an historic occasion witnessed by more than 3,000 area residents eager to see that first official flight land. Actually, the public event was just that: a public event. The pilot, Sid Molloy, made his initial landing several hours in advance of the regularly scheduled mail drop in order to make it more convenient for more people to watch the landing.

Molloy made his first public stop at 8:15 p.m. on that first day of May. The first scheduled northbound airmail drop was more than three hours later. The hour really didn't matter because spectators who witnessed the trial run stayed around for the official inaugural mail plane landing after 11 p.m. There were, in fact, hundreds of spectators still milling around the airstrip at 3 a.m. the next morning awaiting the southbound airmail drop.

Late in the same year, airmail service was extended to Miami; in 1929 Raleigh and Charlotte were added to the mail route landing sites. Two years later, Pitcairn Aviation became Eastern Air Transport and later evolved into Eastern Airlines.

Greensboro through the years hasn't often been able to brag about being ahead of progress in the state's two other major cities, but it was clearly out front in making aviation history with the airmail service.

The first charter flight from the local airport took place nine months prior to the initial mail plane stop, on July 24, 1927. On that date, Henry Rafus, the local airport manager, flew Dr. Herbert Ogburn of Greensboro to New York, a six-hour trip, for a medical emergency. The one-way fare cost $400.

The first commercial passenger service started at the local airport on December 10, 1930, but it was hardly customer friendly. The earliest passenger planes were still designed mostly for mail delivery and had space for only seven paying customers. Passenger space was doubled to 14 when Curtis Condors were placed in service in the spring of 1931. The airport landing strip was sod throughout most of the 1930s until a Franklin Roosevelt New Deal Works Progress Administration (WPA) project in 1937 provided funds for the first paved runways.

The federal grant was obtained for paving the runway after several scary landings that caused the U.S. Department of Commerce to declare the dirt landing strip unsafe. The runway was upgraded again in 1939 after local business leaders advanced the county $67,000 to match another federal grant.

The existing Airport Authority was created legislatively by the N.C. General Assembly in 1941. One of the authority's first acts was to issue revenue bonds that the county used to repay the local businessmen who had two years earlier loaned the money for runway improvements.

The local airport became an important link in United States military efforts during World War II and was, in effect, put under the jurisdiction of the Army Air Corps. In that capacity, the airport served as the aviation facility of the Overseas Replacement Depot (ORD) based in Greensboro and was a refueling stop for the Air Corps Ferry Command. During the war

years, civilian passenger service was virtually eliminated because almost all operations there related to
military purposes.

The first airport authority chairman was Joseph
T. Martin, the manager of the downtown Meyers Department Store. Other original members were Robert
Amos, Ceasar Cone, Charles Kearns, and Russell Hall
Sr. Cone never served as chairman of the authority,
but he didn't need the title to control most of what
went on at the airport in the early days. It was clear
from the beginning that he was the man with the power
because of his domineering personality and blunt talk.
He served 26 years as a member of the airport authority with the title of secretary. No one had more influence over airport matters during his reign, regardless
of titles. Frank is the only other person to serve on the
airport authority as long as Cone did and is one of the
few who ever challenged Cone's directives.

Cone, a member of the Cone textile family,
clashed at one time or another with virtually everyone he dealt with at the airport, including Frank. "He
was tough," Frank said of Cone. "He was very direct,
never very tactful. He wanted things done his way.
Although he was never chairman, he ran the board.
And he was benevolent toward the airport. Cone
bought up a lot of land around the airport and said he
planned to give it to the airport authority. Then he
got upset with the way things were going and we (the
authority) had to buy the land from him. He thought
we were spending too much money and he didn't like
some of the appointments to the authority. That was
just his nature. I never took it personally."

Cone drew public criticism for owning so much
land around the airport when he served on the authority, although he said he was buying it for airport

use and not personal gain. He wanted to prevent development in the area. After Cone left the authority in a pique, the authority obtained court-ordered condemnation in order to buy the land from Cone at prices set by the courts. "Whatever the court said was the fair price was what we paid," former airport executive director Roger Sekadlo said.

Cone, former chairman of what was then family-owned Cone Mills, was also a private pilot who owned a plane, a Challenger biplane. Stories about Cone and his involvement with airport operations are legion, most relating to his power and insistence on doing things his way. He would frequently invite airport staff members to lunch only to spend an afternoon berating them for some action he didn't like or didn't agree with. "I've listened to him for hours, hardly having a chance to say a word," said former Guilford County planning director Lindsey Cox. Cox cited one example of Cone's hard line, even though he had to give up in the end.

Cone opposed a master plan for the airport, preferring to piecemeal the growth and land purchases. In one meeting with a FAA official, Cone stubbornly refused to agree with the need for a long-range plan and continued to grouse about what the federal official was saying.

"Mr. Cone," the FAA spokesman said, "I'm with the federal government and if you don't agree to what we are proposing, I'll withdraw every dime of federal money from this airport." With that, the official turned to county planner Cox and said, "Come on. Let's get out of here."

Cone was livid. But he begrudgingly invited the FAA representative to stay and they agreed on the master plan. He had no other choice.

Frank was named to the airport authority while Cone was still a member in 1962, replacing Russell Hall Sr. at Hall's death. Frank's first confrontation with Cone came shortly afterward when Cone privately insisted that Frank accept the chairmanship. "I declined because at the time I didn't think I had the experience needed for that role," Frank said. "I told Ceasar if he wanted another chairman he ought to take the job. He got pretty angry with me about that. He wanted to run things but do it his way, behind the scenes. My relationship with him was pretty much like his relationship with everybody else: strained. When he disagreed, he did so vehemently. He had a strong desire to carry forward with his own agenda. He was hard to deal with, but we got along and he was very dedicated to progress there.

"He was certainly instrumental in the development of the airport and always carried a great deal of influence in the way the place was run when he was there. But he sincerely felt when he made a decision it was the right one, if not the popular one. He and World War I flying ace and later president of Eastern Airlines Eddie Rickenbacher were great friends. That relationship helped us gain some service from Eastern when we needed it."

Frank once related to a friend an anecdotal encounter he had in a telephone conversation with Cone, who was upset over a pending zoning issue. "I had a 40-minute conversation with Ceasar this morning," Frank told his golfing partner, Ralph D. Stout Sr. "He called me a [vulgar name] and a stupid [vulgar name]. You know, Ralph, I really hate being called stupid." Stout always enjoyed retelling that story.

Frank ultimately, of course, became the Ceasar Cone of the airport authority, in power if not personality. He served on the authority for 29 years from 1962 until 1991. He was chairman from 1972 until he was forced to leave the board in 1991 for what he considers petty political reasons. After a three-year absence, he was reappointed for another three years between 1994 and 1997, then removed again after further political maneuvering by Republican county commissioners.

Airport staff members met Frank's selection as authority chairman in 1972 with varying degrees of enthusiasm and anxiety. They held him in high regard, but some were intimidated by his hard-charging, no-nonsense approach to the job. When he was around, they were all on their best behavior, often scurrying around to make sure they appeared busy, even if they were not, deferring to his power and influence.

"I'll confess I was a little bit frightened when I was asked to be his secretary at the authority after he was named chairman," commented long-time airport office worker Linda Patton. "He was so powerful and influential and I had never dealt much directly

Stanley Frank and his son Bill, May 1957, shortly after Frank learned to pilot his own airplane.

with him. He had always seemed so serious, and the busier he was the happier he was."

Frank early on defused Patton's fears with his subtle sense of humor, shocking her in the process.

"I have only one question," Frank said as he stepped into Patton's airport office the day he was selected as chairman.

"What's that?" she inquired.

"Will you sit on my lap when I ask you to take dictation?" he asked.

"I looked up in shock, not knowing what to say. Then he laughed and said, 'You know I'm kidding, don't you?' That broke the barrier. There was no fear or intimidation after that because of his sincerity, warmth and good humor. He said we'd get along just fine and we did. He was a wonderful chairman, a real gentleman. No one could have been finer or more supportive of this community. His is a pioneering spirit. Since I've known him, he's always had the proper sense of direction for what is right."

As authority chairman, Frank implemented rules for the staff, sometimes rules even he would later agree were too strict. One rule prohibited food in the boardroom. During one stressful evening in 1972 when an attempted hijacking of an airplane by bank robbers was underway, the office staff members wanted to order food and beverages for the employees and law enforcement people working the scene from the board room. Frank said no, the rules prohibited that.

He later called the authority offices from his home and said he was wrong to adhere to such a rule under such circumstances. "I've been talking with Dorothy. She feels I was wrong and you were right," he told Patton. "I agree. Get those people something to eat and drink." The hijacking attempt failed later that night and the workers went home with full stomachs.

When Frank became a member of the airport authority in 1962, there was only one major airline serving the facility and passenger boardings were fewer than 95,000 a year. When he left the board, boardings surpassed one million a year and annual revenue was in excess of $130 million. During his tenure, he constantly worked with commercial airlines to improve and expand passenger service. He was also a strong advocate of freight air service long before it became an accepted means of delivery of goods.

By the beginning of the 21st century, the regional airport had become one of the county's largest employers, pumping millions a year into the local economy. Much of that growth came during Frank's service as chairman of the airport authority board.

Frank's forced departure from the authority was the result of county commissioners imposing term limits on local boards. That move started in the late 1980s while Democrat Dorothy Kearns was commissioner chairperson. Kearns' intentions may have been to make boards more inclusive, but the result has been unproductive political gamesmanship that began after Republicans gained control of the board of commissioners in 1990.

When Republicans took control of the board of commissioners that year, they immediately dumped Frank, a registered Democrat but a fiscal conservative, from the airport authority, naming one of their own in his place.

Guilford County commissioners appoint three airport authority members even though the authority is an independent agency created by state legislation and is not a county governmental unit. The airport receives no local tax money and supports itself through airport revenues.

In removing Frank, Republican commissioners picked their fellow active party member and then fellow commissioner, local businessman Walter Cockerham. "It was a purely political move, in my opinion," Frank said.

When Democrats regained control of the commissioners in 1994, Frank was named to the authority again, replacing Cockerham, but was bumped off in 1997 because Republicans were again in control. Cockerham was once more picked to take his place.

Despite the political musical chairs, despite being part of the Republican coup that forced Frank's departure from the airport authority, Cockerham had high praise for Frank's role in airport growth. "Nobody ever worked harder than Stanley. I know he was personally hurt by being replaced," Cockerham said. "He continues to ask to be of service and I still call on him because I value his advice and counsel. His word is as good as gold."

Frank made it clear he didn't appreciate his treatment in the political sausage grinder. "All that political meddling was unnecessary and never should have happened," Frank said with emphasis. "It started with Dot Kearns and then went from bad to ridiculous under the Republican commissioners and some of their ilk. I was not a political animal and had worked with both parties through the years, based on need of the community and the quality of candidates. I am a registered Democrat but have voted locally for Republicans as often and more often in national elections.

The process and the politics surrounding this issue are really distasteful to me.

"The Republicans were being vindictive without any justification. They were trying to get me for reasons I still don't understand. I was upset and am hurt with the way it was handled. I gave the airport all I had."

Eugene Johnston, an enterprising local businessman and former one-term Republican congressman, succeeded Frank as authority chairman. Johnston, whom Frank called a good authority chairman, didn't participate in removing Frank and, in fact, deplored such political shenanigans.

"The airport authority should never be political," Johnston said. "Political interference hasn't helped. Instead, it has slowed things down. Stanley Frank worked long and hard for the airport and was always straight as an arrow, a very capable business-

Stanley Frank in the cockpit of his first airplane, which he bought for his company in 1957.

man. He never used his position there for personal gain and always put the community and its people first."

Frank's only fault, in Johnston's view, is that he sometimes took on too many duties. "A person needs to decide how many fights he can put his dog into. Sometimes I felt that Stanley had too many simultaneous dog fights, too many projects going for his own good." It was Johnston who pushed to ensure that Frank received at least some of the credit he deserved for his years of service to the airport when Johnston arranged for the authority's meeting room to be named for Frank.

The Stanley Frank Boardroom was officially dedicated March 28, 1991. A plaque there honors Frank for "service, loyalty and dedication toward growth and the future" of the airport.

The only other thing at the airport with Frank's name attached has been a hot dog, but that was all in fun. When the new terminal opened, concession prices shot skyward and, as a joke, someone named the $3 hot dog the Frank frankfurter.

Once Frank became authority chairman in 1972, after Cone left the board, he quickly yet smoothly became the driving force although his influence had also been growing during his first decade as an authority member. He spent countless hours working for the airport's orderly growth and planning for its progress. No chairman has given so much time and energy as Frank.

It was Frank who pleaded with Guilford County Commissioners on December 17, 1973, against rezoning land near the airport for residential use. The land in question was once a farm owned by former Jefferson

Standard Insurance president Ralph Price. Frank argued against residential zoning because he said the airport would eventually need to expand: adding runways with residences so close to the noise cone would be controversial.

Commissioners, with Republicans in control, rejected Frank's pleas on a 3-to-2 vote. Frank's prophecy has proved true. The rezoned land has become the upscale 700-acre Cardinal residential subdivision and by the beginning of the 21st century had become embroiled in exactly the kind of unfriendly neighborhood debate Frank predicted because of the proposed Federal Express distribution center at the airport.

The existing airport terminal was opened in 1982, but it was a master plan on the drawing boards for 20 years that brought it about — with Frank involved every step of the way. He was a member of the authority when the plan was conceived and was chairman when it was carried out.

Frank also pushed to expand the authority membership in 1985 to ensure that Winston-Salem and Forsyth County would have representation. That was one of his many efforts to expand the concept and reality of regionalism, both for fairness and more orderly economic growth.

Using his business acumen and ties to financial institutions through First Boston, Frank helped secure favorable interest rates for authority bonds to build the new terminal, which carried a $65 million price tag. He arranged that favorable rate with the aid of his friend Tom Bradshaw of Raleigh, former head of the North Carolina Department of Transportation, who was then an investment banker with First Boston. Bradshaw was in that job, in part, because of Frank.

Frank and Bradshaw had become friends earlier when they worked on state government issues involving highways and aviation. When Bradshaw was looking for a different career after his service in state government, he followed Frank's suggestion to check out First Boston. "Stanley helped me get some interviews with First Boston because of his connections with the company and the respect company officials had for him," Bradshaw said. "I owe a great deal of allegiance to him."

Frank seemed, as Bradshaw has said, to adopt the airport as a member of his family during his many years of leadership responsibility there. He not only was out front in helping ensure the building of the new terminal and improved passenger service, but he has also kept up with routine items even down to restroom maintenance.

One example illustrates the point. During a par-

Delivery Day, April 1957. Stanley Frank (left) accepts delivery of his first company airplane, a Beechcraft, purchased in Wichita, Kansas. With him are Ken Brugh (right), a private air service operator, and Jack Pepper.

ticular visit to the terminal, Frank expressed frustration because a uniformed worker didn't restock paper towels in the men's room, as Frank had recommended. He was told that the worker was an airline employee, not an airport authority worker. "Well, then get somebody to put the towels in there," Frank chastised an authority official. It was done.

"He was forever monitoring something," former operations manager Floyd McKenzie said. "He was involved in everything and always felt the airport came first."

Frank, for example, directed that airport staff members use pagers in order to communicate better and provide more efficient customer service. Frank himself carried a pager because he wanted to stay in close touch with operations. To help break up tensions during stressful periods, the staff sometimes sent bogus messages to each other's pagers, until the pranks backfired with Frank on the receiving end.

Once when an employee was jokingly attempting to leave a massage parlor phone number on a colleague's pager, he mistakenly left the number on Frank's pager. Frank immediately returned the phone call only to discover he was being offered an Oriental massage by a woman with a foreign-sounding, yet sensuous, voice.

"He started asking what the hell was going on," McKenzie said. "He couldn't figure out how he got such a telephone number on his pager. We told him it must have been a wrong number and he should just ignore it. We never told him what really happened."

When he wasn't dealing with mundane airport items, Frank was engaged in promoting the facility and working for its development.

"I guess maybe I was involved in Triadism before anyone knew what the word meant," he said.
"There is no reason why the cities shouldn't maintain
their own identities, but they've also got to work together if any of them expect to succeed. My primary
responsibility as chairman of the airport authority was
to see the airport grow and expand. But I also felt I
had a very definite responsibility to see that the region developed as it should. Cities ought to be com-
petitive, but we've all got to work together if it [or-
derly growth] is going to work at all."

When Frank wanted to include more Winston-
Salem representatives in airport matters, he arranged
for Forsyth leaders to take a bus tour of the new facilities. At a later time when he needed Standard & Poor
and Moody's bond rating agencies to see the potential
of a new terminal, he flew them over the Piedmont
region for a personal look. When he wanted to protect
the airport property against municipal interference,
he went to the state legislature to secure passage of
laws prohibiting city annexation.

When Frank wanted Eastern Airline's support
for the terminal expansion, critical because the airline was then the largest carrier, he brought in President Col. Frank Borman, the former astronaut, for a
tour and dinner. After his visit, Borman became a major
proponent of the new terminal plans. Once Borman
signed on, other airlines fell quickly in line. "He was
very cooperative and very helpful," Frank said of the
former astronaut.

Frank even created the present name for the
airport. It may not be the best name, he conceded,
but it was better than the many earlier ones that tended
to slight one of the region's cities. And with the present
name, at least there is less jealousy among the cities,

he contended.

"The name just came out of a brainstorm one day," he said. "It sort of caught on." Evolving from Lindley Field at Friendship, to Tri-City Airport, to Greensboro-High Point Airport (after Winston reneged on the original pledge of support) to the Greensboro-High Point-Winston-Salem Airport, to Regional Airport, the current Piedmont Triad International is inclusive but not unwieldy.

"The earlier and varied names were too long with all the cities included," he said. "Airline representatives wouldn't include all the city names in their announcements and there was always concern over which city names were used or omitted in on-board messages. Nothing seemed to work right. Charlotte and Raleigh had just one or two city names to deal with. People were always raising hell here because one city name was always left out. I wanted a Triad name to avoid the bitter feelings over city names. So one day I came up with the Piedmont Triad International name. I got a lot of heat for including 'international,' but that has to do with freight service. We have international freight." In the summer of 2001, the airport also got passenger service outside the United States with some flights to Canada.

Frank's renaming plan hasn't worked exactly as he intended. Airline employees still tend to refer to the airport as "Greensboro" rather than PTI.

If there is sadness with Frank involving the airport, it's that he is no longer considered an active participant. He clearly misses that opportunity.

"There comes a point in life where you find you are being consulted less and you have to carry a smaller stick," he said as far back as a 1991 magazine interview.

Those personal feelings were even more pronounced in a conversation he had with Marlene Chernitski, who served Frank for a decade as a secretary at the airport. "I hope you never have to know what it's like when they don't need you anymore," Cherniski quoted him as saying after he was removed from the authority board.

But Frank carries a card in his wallet that looks at the other side of issues. "When life deals you lemons, make lemonade and sell it for a profit," the card reads.

Frank was still making lemonade past his middle 80s. The profit he was making was for the community. "Besides," he said, "I'm still available."

If the airport calls, Stanley Frank is ready for the takeoff.

9

Stanley & the Generals

For a fellow who hardly knew the difference between a penalty box and a petunia, Stanley Frank may have seemed to some sports fans an unlikely part owner of a professional hockey team.

But not to worry. A business is a business. You learn as you go; you help it along as you go along. That was the Frank way. The aim of any good business is to please customers, provide a useful service, and make a profit.

That's what Frank had done when he took control of a faltering rendering plant and that's what he and his partners did with their fledgling sports team. In truth, though, Frank really never made any money off hockey, and his partners didn't make much either, because that was not their intent.

The team, the Greensboro Generals, actually cost Frank money, even though he has no idea how much because he never added up personal expenses. His purpose was to do something positive for his community as he helped spread pleasure to thousands of customers — in this case, fans — who seemed to appreciate his efforts.

"I didn't know anything about hockey when I got involved with the team," Frank conceded. "All I knew about ice skating was that I had done a little of that on public ponds as a kid growing up in New York. But I feel we did provide a service to the city and entertainment to the fans."

Indeed.

The year was 1959. The City of Greensboro had just opened its new coliseum on West Lee Street after several failed attempts to locate the facility in or near downtown. Critics of the arena said it would be a perpetual drain on municipal finances, a red ink white elephant.

A handful of businessmen set out to prove the critics wrong. Leading the way were Stanley Frank and Carson Bain. Bain was the show horse, the man out front dealing with public support. Frank was the workhorse, the man pulling the plow behind the scenes.

Both men had been proponents of the new coliseum and adjoining War Memorial Auditorium, and both were determined to help ensure success of the facilities. They and others discussed options toward the best and fastest way to achieve their goal.

They agreed on the need for an anchor drawing card and began searching out sports franchises. Their options were limited, of course, because they needed an indoor sport. College basketball had not yet become an addiction for area fans as it would decades later and professional basketball was then still a northern, big city form of entertainment.

The coliseum was equipped to create an ice rink, but families of skaters would hardly produce needed income, even if they came to skate. The ice was there, but there was not much use for it.

"What we need," Southern-born Bain said during one of his brainstorming sessions with Frank "is a hockey team." It was an idea worth discussing, although Frank wasn't sure his friend was really serious. In fact, Bain wasn't fully convinced himself. Hockey was pretty much a foreign sport in the South in those post-war days, although Charlotte had a team at the time. But both men knew they had to come up with something or the coliseum critics would just keep on criticizing.

From that discussion, the Greensboro Generals were eventually born. "We did it for the city and for the coliseum," Frank said with full agreement from Bain. "We wanted something to help the coliseum succeed, to provide entertainment for citizens and revenue for the facility."

Bain had established himself in the city as a public relations whiz. He was always an out-front, look-at-the-positive-side promoter who had learned leadership through the Jaycees and was in the early stages of a budding political career that would later put him in the mayor's office following service on the county board of commissioners. If there was a community project going on, Bain was more than likely attached to the front of it.

Frank was more reluctant to be a focal point on projects, but he was no less enthusiastic and people were already beginning to look to him as the person who could get things done quietly. He has successfully carried that banner for another 40-plus years.

The two began scouting for a hockey team, although neither really knew exactly what they would do if they found one. Either Frank or Bain — neither can remember which one — heard about a defunct team in Troy, Ohio, that could be bought for $25,000.

Neither man was willing to commit the personal resources to purchase the team outright, but they had contacts with and the respect of the Greensboro business community. They went to friends in town and in short order had enough pledges in hand to make the purchase.

The only investor outside Greensboro was golf legend Sam Snead, a buddy of Bain. Investors who made up the original stockholder board of directors with Frank and Bain were Sidney Stern Jr., Hargrove "Skipper" Bowles, Kelly Bowles, A.A. (Red) Brame, Patrick Calhoun, Dr. Edward Carr, Lawrence Cohen, Norman Curtis, Walter King Jr., James Perrin, William Ragsdale Jr., John Rendleman, Harold Smith, William Stern and Dr. C. T. Whittington. Other early investors were Blake Clark and Ann Cone.

Cone, a sports enthusiast, was the wife of textile executive and former mayor Benjamin Cone. The only woman to join the ownership group in the early years, she took a particularly personal interest and became one of the biggest boosters. She arranged housing for many of the players in the homes of her northwest Greensboro neighbors and friends.

"This was just one of her unusual investments," her son Ben Cone said of his mother. "She loved hockey and was especially concerned about the personal lives of the players," most of whom were Canadian and had little or no knowledge of southern customs. Dr. Whittington served as the team physician in addition to having a slice of the ownership.

Frank, Bain, and their local associates didn't exactly get a hockey team with their original investment, as they had intended. What they actually bought was a stack of equipment: pucks, sticks, gloves and masks. There were no players.

"That's when the work really started," Bain said. He and Frank had to find and sign players, no easy task for a couple of amateurs in professional sports. Bain began his customary public relations approach of promoting the idea of hockey to townspeople while Frank began the arduous task of player contract negotiations. Frank and Bain hired a series of general managers to run the team in the early days, but after several changes in personnel they changed direction. Frank took over most of the player management duties. He became the point person, working diligently in the trenches to find young men who knew how to play the game and who might be interested in coming to and playing in a southern town that knew more about grits than goalies. The other investors just hoped for the best. While none of them really expected to make much money from their ownership, they put the burden on Frank and Bain to see that they wouldn't lose too much.

Frank and Bain made a successful management team. Bain was team president; Frank, vice president. Ken Wilson, the only team official with any background in hockey, was the first of three general managers. Roly McLenahan was the first coach.

After assuming management duties, Frank went after hockey players — literally — just as hard as he did raw materials for his rendering business several miles east of the coliseum. He established contacts with hockey teams in this country and in Canada. He became good friends with Tommy Ivan, who was the general manager of the Chicago Black Hawks, and Charlie Kunkle, a Duke University graduate and later a member of the U.S. Olympic Committee, who owned the Johnstown Jets.

Ivan routinely advised Frank about prospective players, those who were good enough for the professional sport but not quite good enough for the better hockey leagues. "He gave us some players," Frank said of Ivan. "He did a great job for us and helped a lot." Kunkle worked with Frank on ways to manage a team and run a successful hockey franchise. The two frequently exchanged ideas on business decisions.

Frank became, in effect, the general of the Generals. He used his company airplane to fly to Canada and regions of the United States to recruit and sign players. He was the team owners' sole negotiator, and a tenacious one, too. What he wanted in contracts was usually what he got.

A half dozen of the original Generals players remained in Greensboro after their playing days ended. They liked the city and respected Frank for his business approach to the team despite the hard bargains he drove with contracts. He was tough, they said, but always fair and honest. A few of the former players were employed during the off season and after hockey retirement by some of the original Generals investors in their private companies.

Frank and players wrangled over a few dollars a week in contract negotiations. Frank took that approach, not just to penny pinch although he was tight with a dollar, but because surplus team resources were most often not plentiful.

He once temporarily lost a player over a $10 a week dispute on a new contract. Refusing to give up, Frank flew his company plane to Canada to close the deal. The player was Pat Kelly, one of the better team members. Frank wanted to cut Kelly's pay by $10 when his contract for $165 a week came up for renewal because the team had made very little money the previous season. Kelly rejected the pay cut and refused to sign a new contract, leaving town for his native Canada.

"I went home," Kelly said. "I'm driving toward St. Thomas, Ontario, when the police pulled me over and said there's a guy chasing me and needs to talk with me. It was Stanley Frank. He flew to Canada to negotiate that $10 pay cut and somehow found out where I was. He was a determined taskmaster but always fair. If he could give you a higher salary he would. He never promised what he couldn't give."

Frank's trip to Canada paid off. Kelly signed the new contract and played for the Generals for four more years, including the 1962-63 season when the team won the league championship. Kelly was later traded to the New Jersey Devils with the Generals getting three players in exchange. Kelly is one of the Generals who remained in the South. He now lives in Charlotte and is involved in the administrative side of another hockey league.

"Professional sports is not always filled with people of integrity," Frank's friend Charlie Kunkle said from his home in Pennsylvania. "But Stanley is an exception, a man whose word is as good as gold, a person whose integrity is unimpeachable. He never violated any rules, he never cut corners and he ran the Generals as a business. He was outspoken in his efforts to structure the team and the sport with integrity. He spent his own money doing that because he wanted to do the right thing and help the community.

"He maintained a well run organization, taking a big risk to do what he did. He has done a lot for his community and the hockey team effort is just one of his worthy endeavors. If I had to pick my own fraternity of fine people I have known through the years, Stanley would be among the first chosen and would always remain a member."

Kunkle said he received as much education in running a hockey team as he did during his years as a Duke student where he graduated in 1936. "Stanley was among those giving good advice," he said. Kunkle knew hockey, but Frank knew business. Each benefited from the other's knowledge.

During those successful years, however, Frank established himself as a knowledgeable person of hockey as well as business. His efforts drew the attention and respect of hockey team owners in other cities. In 1969, Frank was offered the job as commissioner of the Eastern Hockey League. He turned down the job.

The early days of the Generals proved Frank and Bain right in their assessment of the value of the team to the new coliseum, which at the time could seat 9,000 fans. The arena was seldom full for home games, but on weekends crowds were plentiful, and occasionally all seats were sold. The team made money for the coliseum. Fans were upset when they couldn't get tickets for the seats they wanted. The team always made a profit, albeit sometimes a small one.

Team owners had a signed agreement with the coliseum that set a fee for use of the facility, although neither Frank nor Bain could remember the exact amount. In fact, the coliseum managers more or less determined the revenue; they handled ticket sales and provided team owners with a percentage. "We were not in it for the money," Bain said, explaining the financial arrangement with the coliseum, which also reaped profits from parking and concessions. "We pretty much accepted what the coliseum folks said and took the revenue they gave us. They got theirs first."

Enthusiasm of fans intensified with the growing rivalry between the Generals and the Charlotte Checkers. Each team had at least one player to spark fan fury. John Brophy played the villain for the Checkers and Don Carter filled that role for the Generals. Clashes on the ice between those two helped bring out fans.

"The team was a valuable asset to the coliseum and we generated a lot of revenue," said then coliseum manager Bob Kent. "Stanley Frank was involved in every aspect of the team, very much in tune with what was going on. He was their top person, sort of the governor or the general. He had a good sense of the business side, which helped the team succeed."

Hockey games became major social events for Greensboro in the early years. Thousands of fans regularly made home games a time for fun evenings. Season ticket holders among Greensboro's more affluent citizens had a special reason to attend games: they had their own little private club, the "Generals Room," where they could partake of food and beverages (strong and weak) during timeouts and before and after games.

Success lasted more than a decade from that inaugural season in 1959. But by the beginning of the second decade of ownership, investor Sidney Stern Jr., Frank's personal friend and business lawyer suggested the stockholders look for someone else to take control. Stern and several other stockholders wanted to keep the team intact but were interested in getting out of ownership. Frank wasn't among those who wanted to give up control, but he didn't object to shopping for potential buyers.

That, though, was the beginning of the end for the team that had been so successful.

Bain was assigned the task of seeking new owners. He learned of interest from Jim Gardner, a state Republican Party golden boy from Rocky Mount, North Carolina, who had served one term in Congress and had been a candidate for governor. Gardner was part owner of the Carolina Cougars of the American Basketball Association, which split its home games between the coliseums in Greensboro and Charlotte.

Bain, however, had little personal faith in Gardner or his ability to purchase the team. Bain had heard things about past Gardner business deals that he didn't like. "I didn't really trust him," Bain said. "But I met with him over lunch. I told him the team was for sale but there would be restrictions — no credit extended and no personal check accepted. I told Gardner we wanted cash up front. When he heard that, he got up and walked out. End of discussion."

While Gardner was personally out of the picture as a potential owner, the Cougars were not. Tedd Munchak, another Cougar owner, purchased majority interest in the Generals in the spring of 1971. He paid $100,000 for the franchise and agreed to pay the coliseum $54,000 a year in rent, exorbitant figures that helped drive him into deep debt.

The original stockholders and the coliseum officials were delighted with those inflated figures. Stockholders were able to gain from their original investment and earn a profit, except for Frank who had spent more of his own money on the team than he recouped. Frank never charged the team any fee for his frequent airplane trips to Canada and other cities to recruit players or for other out-of-pocket expenses.

Munchak was a high-flying, fast-dealing businessman from Rome, Georgia, who was involved in the furniture, carpet and cattle business. After purchasing the Cougars and the Generals, he publicly promised to establish himself as a big-time sports entrepreneur. He talked a better game than he played. His business dealings were frequently on a roller coaster ride and his financial arrangements with at least one local person turned sour in a hurry.

Norman Curtis, one of the original Generals' owners and partner in his family's Curtis Packing Company, was one who engaged in some cattle trading with Munchak. As part of their association, he became a part owner and general manager of the hockey team. Curtis' business dealings with Munchak proved to be an expensive lesson. "I lost about $90,000 in my dealings with him," Curtis said. "Munchak was a very bright fellow, but he had a lot of personal problems," including, according to Curtis, excessive consumption of alcohol.

The Generals rapidly fell on hard times under the Munchak ownership, and soon a series of revolving door owners took over. In the 18 seasons the Generals played in Greensboro, they had four different sets of owners, three of them in the final five years. None succeeded the way the original owners did.

Three years into Munchak's ownership in February 1975, the team was in deep financial debt to Greensboro businessman Eugene Johnston, among others. Munchak owed Johnston's company, Fisher-Harrison Printing, for printing work and other services. Johnston, an astute businessman with formal training in both law and accounting (and later a Congressman), was fed up with extending credit. He decided to take action.

Johnston tried several avenues of collection, none too successful; in April of that year he was still owed $40,000. "I soon determined that everything he (Munchak) owned had a lien on it." Johnston said. "I tried to take over some of his assets, but the only thing that wasn't already pledged for a debt was the Generals' franchise. I don't know if you can just take over a franchise, but that's exactly what I did and no one challenged it."

So Eugene Johnston became a reluctant owner of a faltering hockey team in July 1975. "What I know about hockey you could write on the back of your hand," Johnston told a newspaper reporter when he assumed ownership. "My interest is to preserve an asset for Greensboro."

He also made other comments for public consumption, statements about how great it was to own a hockey team, but he had to bite his lip as he spoke. What he had was a sports franchise that he wanted to unload.

"There I was owning this team and I kept saying it was great," Johnston said in the fall of 2000 about his brief ownership. "But I went to a couple of owner meetings and learned that the only team in the league making money was Salem and yet owners were talking about raising salaries. I knew pretty quickly that I was in the wrong business in the wrong league."

Johnston came up with a new strategy. He

adopted the Tom Sawyer approach about whitewashing the fence. He figured, he said, if he kept publicly proclaiming how happy he was with the team someone else would step forward and offer to buy it. The plan worked. After a month of ownership, Johnston found a willing buyer in August 1975.

A group of Greensboro businessmen led by Richard Maxwell approached Johnston about buying the team. Well, yes, Johnston said with a serious tone of reservation, he'd consider an offer, claiming with a straight face that he wasn't overly anxious to sell.

"Boy, was I happy," Johnston said 25 years after closing the deal that he was so delighted to make. "I sold the team for $50,000, which was enough to pay off my debts. I licensed the team to them and got out of it."

Maxwell thought he had made a sweetheart deal, but he soon learned differently. "I later learned that Johnston could hardly contain his enthusiasm, despite his seeming hesitation. He was tickled that someone would actually want the team and would give him cash for it," Maxwell said.

Maxwell, a successful real estate developer who got his start in that business with the help of Stanley Frank, was one of six owners who bought the Generals. The other investors forming what was called the Piedmont Partnership were Ken Lewis Sr., Maurice Miller, Conway Owings, Dick Michaud and Carl Sheer.

"We had visions of making big bucks," Maxwell said. "It didn't work out that way."

The new owners had what they felt was an iron-clad plan for success. Shortly before buying the Generals, some of them had invested in the Piedmont Sports Arena, a public ice skating facility on Norwalk

Street, off West Wendover Avenue, several miles west of the coliseum. The skating arena was wildly popular in the beginning, but it didn't last.

With shrinking fan support for the Generals at the coliseum under the Munchak ownership, the new owners decided to move the team to the 3,500-seat Sports Arena for home games as one means of reducing expenses. They built player locker rooms and acquired beer concessions at the new location.

The timing was dismal. As the investors were pouring money into the arena, the national gas crunch hit. Fans couldn't get gasoline to drive to work and other essential trips, much less to drive to social events. There were other problems, too. Some newly recruited hockey players developed bad reputations. "The newer players were dirty and had women hanging on," Maxwell said. "The result wasn't what we had hoped it would be." People stopped coming to games. Losses continued to mount.

"The team became a financial drain on us, a real drag," Maxwell said. "We folded the team in 1977 and went into default. Each investor lost about $100,000 before the team was dissolved."

Lewis called the venture a business proposition that just didn't work out. "I'm thankful that all my business efforts didn't turn out like that one," he said.

Johnston, after selling the team, tried to warn the new owners of their pending pitfall.

Johnston called minor league hockey a "nickel and dime" business fraught with problems. He also advised the new owners to call on Frank for his expertise in running the team, advice that apparently wasn't taken. In an August 15, 1975, letter to new owner Conway Owings, Johnston wrote:

"The sports arena doesn't make economic sense unless you have ancillary sources of income. You and Dick (Maxwell) are competent businessmen, but you are going to have to pool your collective talents and energies to make it work. I hope you will resort to Stanley's advice and counsel. He carries a good deal of respect in the hockey business. I want to do whatever I can to keep you from stepping in any economic potholes. You are going to have to watch every nickel and dime. By mismanagement, this team can cost you both your business reputations."

Johnston's words, of course, would become more prophetic than perhaps even he realized at the time.

Once the Generals folded, the team's owners tried to salvage something from their sports arena investment. After giving up on the team and allowing the building to sit vacant for three years, the owners found a buyer who promised to turn it into a high-class nightclub with top-flight entertainment. But that venture failed just like the hockey team.

The building became the *Moulin Rouge,* with new owners, The Valhalla Entertainment Corporation, promising big things along with their big investment. The nightclub opened on March 7, 1980, with Barbara Eden ("I Dream of Jeannie") as the headliner. She appeared in a sheer, silver-spangled gown that was a clear-cut crowd pleaser to the more than 800 diners on the main floor and the 100 on the three tiers where hockey fans once sat.

The club owners heaped fanfare far and wide about upcoming entertainers, but there was more fanfare than fans. Owners produced Tom Jones and Roger Miller after Eden's initial performance, but the announced arrival of Red Foxx, Bob Hope and Captain and Tennille never materialized.

Four months after opening with all the hoopla, the nightclub was more than $1.5 million in debt, and First Home Federal had foreclosed on a $552,000 mortgage.

The club closed at the end of July. The building has since been sold and used for private business. Hockey would eventually return to Greensboro, but not for a long time and not with the original enthusiasm that Frank, Bain and their fellow investors produced.

•

While the latter years of the original Generals' existence in Greensboro were traumatic, that was not the case when Frank and Bain and their group owned the team. Friendships formed during those years still exist. Former players recruited by Frank speak kindly of their relationship with the man who brought them here and negotiated their contracts.

In a "turn back the clock night," members of the 1959 Generals team were honored in the spring of 1995 during a game between the Greensboro Monarchs and Charlotte Checkers.

Generals players receiving special tribute that night were Don Carter, Cam Colborne, Mike Conroy, Howie Heggedal, Ron Hindson, Pat Kelly, Butch MacKay, Ron Muir, John Murray, Brian Randall, Stu Roberts, Ron Spong, Harvard Turnbull, John Voss, Bob Wright, Bill Young and Ron Quenville.

"I quite honestly wasn't too crazy about him at first," Brian (Butch) MacKay said of Frank. "He was a tough negotiator and kind of brash. It also was some-

The Greensboro Generals, team of 1960-61. Seated in the front row center is Carson Bain, team president, who with Stanley Frank led efforts to buy and form a hockey team for Greensboro. Bain, later a Greensboro mayor, was the primary public relations spokesman for the team. Frank was the contract negotiator, and according to the players, a tough one.

thing of a cultural shock coming to this area of the country from Canada. But over time I learned to respect Stanley Frank and realized he was doing what he did to help the community. He did all the work in the trenches and is responsible for the success of the team. He is one of the most respected people I know. He's like old Popeye. He is what he is. If he told you something, that was it. You didn't have to worry that it would be done because it would be done. He is certainly one of my heroes."

"I used to bounce around between Stanley Frank and Carson Bain," said retired player Ron Muir. "Carson would just smile, but Stanley was tough, a firm negotiator and a good businessman. He took good care of the team even as he made sure all the pennies were counted. He became a very good friend and still is."

"There is absolutely nothing pretentious about him," former player Harvard Turnbull said of Frank.

"He's a down to earth guy, always fair to everyone. A lot of team owners treated players unfairly, but Stanley never did. He had a great financial sense and always did what was right. I signed my first contract sitting on his porch and I never regretted it."

"Stanley could take garbage and turn it into gold," said retired Generals player John Murray. "He was as enthusiastic as anyone on the team and he surely did know how to manage a dollar."

Frank took the games as seriously as he did the contract negotiations. His enthusiastic involvement in one game was more than player Don Carter could take. "Stanley was really into the play, and Carter had had enough of his coaching from the stands," Murray said. "Carter threw a cup of water in his face. It was great."

Players admired Frank for his energy and his continuing support despite his hard lines on contract renewal. They also teased him because of his owner-ship of the rendering business. "On road trips, if we'd see a dead animal lying in the road, we'd all say 'Call Stanley,'" former player Pat Kelly said.

Former player Stu Roberts and his wife Amanda have remained friends with Frank and his wife since Roberts' playing days in the middle and late 1960s. "They're wonderful people," Amanda Roberts said. "Stu and I admire both of them greatly." (The Rob-erts' daughter has also made a name for herself here. Jennifer Michelle Roberts was chosen Miss North Caro-lina in 1996 after being chosen as both Miss Guilford County and Miss Thomasville. She is now Jennifer Bad-ger and is married to a medical student.)

Bain said Frank wasn't especially excited about forming a hockey team in Greensboro when it was first mentioned. But once he realized this endeavor would be good for the city, he jumped in with both feet. "That's just the way he is," Bain said. "He has great principles. Once he grabs something, he owns it and won't stop. He went head over heels for the Generals and is a prime reason the team succeeded while our original group owned it. Some people have the ability to be generous with their time and talents and don't do it. Stanley has the ability and he does it."

The Generals team was just one of many community endeavors that Bain hooked Frank up with to make things better for Greensboro.

Chapter 22

The pending prison sale. However, could no longer afford differentiated to latter vault of Carolina By-Products that began in 1980. A series of subsequent rules and new ownership changes ultimately meant that Frank, his two sons and other top company officials would all leave. Frank retired in early 1988. Oldest son Bill was fired shortly afterwards and youngest son Barry resigned, all within the first months of 1988.

That left the Franks worried and wondering what might happen to the enterprise they had worked so hard to build. Regrettably, some of their worst fears turned into reality in the decade after they severed their ties with company operations.

Frank had given each of his two sons 22.5 percent of the company ownership in 1965 during the middle of the IRS harangue. Because of their relatively young ages — Bill was 24 and Barry 20 — Frank put their shares in a trust. That decision had no impact on the tax controversy.

Frank and his sons were the sole stockholders in Carolina By-Products until the chemical division, Chemol, was opened in the midst of the IRS battle. Frank offered three other company officials — Chemol president Len Anderson, Carolina By-Products president Fred Schuster, and sales manager Tom McNulty — the opportunity to own stock in the chemical division. Frank later repurchased their shares before he sold the company to Kane-Miller.

Earlier, in the late 1950s, Frank had initiated a profit sharing plan for company employees. He did that before most Southern companies had such programs and certainly much sooner than most small companies began similar practices. Any employee with 30 months employment was eligible for a percentage of

10

Civic Works & Civility

It has been jokingly said that Stanley Frank's long list of community-wide civic endeavors in Greensboro actually began because he was such a poor golfer. That is, of course, an exaggerated version of his golf game and an understatement of his community service.

But it makes for an amusing story. His golf game isn't really *that* bad.

The most significant part of the story, hyperbole aside, is that Frank did pick up the civic torch and has carried it proudly for more than half a century, into and beyond his middle 80s as the new century began.

Frank's long-time friend and civic partner Carson Bain has over several decades spread the anecdotal tale about community good works and golf. Exaggerated though the tale is, Bain obviously enjoyed telling it. His version goes like this:

"Sidney Stern Jr. called me one day and asked if I could get Stanley appointed to some committees and get him involved in some worthy projects in the county," Bain explained with a mischievous grin.

"Why do you want me to do that?" Bain said he asked Stern.

"Well," Stern was alleged to have said, "there must be something Stanley can do better than he can play golf."

Regardless of precisely what was said in that telephone call or how serious Stern might have been about Frank's golf scores, Stern knew well what Frank could do, on or off the golf course. And he knew Bain had political and civic connections to make good use of Frank's high energy level, his strength as a businessman and his ability to communicate well as a way of getting things done.

For more than 40 years until his death, Stern was Frank's personal attorney and one of his closest friends. They met shortly after Frank came to Greensboro in 1936 and were within four months of the same age, each born in 1914. They and their wives frequently traveled together and worked closely during the formative years of Frank's rendering company development and his civic endeavors.

They also played golf together at least once a week for decades. Their games were great relaxation outlets for the pair who dedicated so much time and serious attention to work as well as to community projects. One major weakness in their golf game, however, was that they didn't always concentrate on scores. Most of their time on the golf course was spent discussing business or other matters not related to putts or tee shots.

"Stanley never has taken the game of golf too seriously," Bain said in an assessment echoed by numerous Frank friends and associates. "He uses the game to talk about business and important community issues as well as to get to know more people. He and

Sidney and I used to play a lot of golf. We were all just duffers, but we had a lot of fun and a lot to talk about."

"I suspect that Carson made up that little story about Sidney, Stanley, and golf," Stern's widow, Kay, said with a chuckle. "Sidney, of course, knew of Stanley's unbounded energy and he simply wanted to get Stanley involved in more community work. Sidney felt Stanley would use his strength to work for the benefit of a lot of people. Sidney also helped get Stanley involved in work at Temple Emanuel. Dorothy Frank was very pleased that Sidney got her husband into the work of the Temple."

Frank, while not as active as some members of that Reformed Jewish congregation in downtown Greensboro, said his faith has helped teach him tolerance and understanding of people sometimes left behind for no reason other than religious beliefs or ethnic background. Those feelings have also played a role in his desire for active community involvement. He understood what it was like to be left out or in the minority.

His religious affiliation once temporarily blocked his membership in a Guilford County so-

Stanley Frank (right) and his long-time corporate and personal lawyer Sidney Stern, Jr. Stern initiated efforts to get Frank involved in civic and community service in Greensboro. They were close friends and golfing partners, playing every week for decades.

cial club.

In 1950, shortly after moving to the Sedgefield neighborhood off High Point Road, Frank asked the procedure for joining the Sedgefield Country Club, in which members of the Jewish Cone family were already enrolled. The response was not encouraging.

"I was not formally denied membership, but it was made clear to me that it might not be wise to apply." Frank explained. "No one told me directly that I would be turned down because I was a Jew, but that was the clear signal. I didn't pursue it at the time. Later I was invited by some members to join the club and have enjoyed many pleasurable times there through the years. I've had no concerns about discrimination since that initial incident. The subject of my faith has never been mentioned again."

On another occasion, Frank and some friends ran head-on into the fact that the dining area at the Greensboro Country Club had never served dinner to a racial minority. Frank said he and his dinner partners didn't intentionally set out to change that policy, but they did exactly that without public notice on a quiet evening during the 1974 NCAA basketball tournament in Greensboro.

Multiple big time sports celebrities were in town for the tournament. One of the celebrities was Chicago Bears running back Gayle Sayers. Frank was one of Sayers' tournament hosts and, following a social hour at the home of attorney Henry Isaacson, Frank suggested the group have dinner at the Greensboro Country Club. The decision raised questions in the minds of some present at the social hour because they knew the club dining room was segregated, but no one openly raised the issue.

"We wondered that might happen when we got there," Isaacson said. "We got to the club where we met Bill Black at the bar. He greeted Sayers and all of us warmly, kissed Sayers' wife on the cheek and we proceeded into the dining room for dinner. What happened was nothing. Dinner was served. No one ever publicly raised a question or even an eyebrow. The evening was delightful." And the Greensboro Country Club dining room has been integrated ever since.

Frank said the subject of race never entered his thinking when he suggested dinner there. He wanted a good meal for his guest, who happened to be black as well as a national sports hero. "I didn't do anything unusual," he said. "We just had dinner. If anyone deserves any special credit for leading the way that night, it was Billy Black. He was in charge once we got there. I never thought about the race issue because to me it wasn't an issue."

No one has ever been able to say with certainty whether dinner was served so casually that night to Frank and his friends because Sayers was a sports hero. Would the same thing likely have occurred regardless of the minority guest's identity? No black had actually been denied service prior to that night because none had ever been a guest there — until Frank escorted Sayers.

Whatever the reason, Frank said, "It was the right thing to do, the natural thing as far as I was concerned, then and now."

The initial indirect rejection of his membership in the Sedgefield Club and the anxiety over whether Sayers would be welcomed at the Greensboro Country Club, Frank said, made him believe even more strongly that people should be treated equally and fairly. He has worked through his years of civic and community activities to ensure that would happen.

In October 1974, the local chapter of the National Conference of Christians and Jews chose Frank for its brotherhood award. Among the public accolades for Frank on that occasion was his dedication to principles and ideals of humanity and his contribution to the better understanding among people of different races and backgrounds.

Race issues, religious prejudice and golf scores aside, it is a fact that Stern made an official request of Bain in the middle 1950s to find a way to make better and broader use of Frank's ability to get things done. And it didn't take long for the effort to bear fruit.

Bain didn't seek out any cushion appointments either. His first selection for Frank was political red meat. Bain was a county commissioner at the time, and he and his colleagues had just approved a politically explosive countywide zoning ordinance. Farmers and other rural landowners that had been accustomed to full unconditional use of their land were building up strong defenses against the new regulations.

Commissioners needed a peacemaker. Bain quickly concluded Frank was the man to fill that role.

Frank had earlier served as chairman of the neighborhood Sedgefield Zoning Commission and Bain seized on that experience plus Frank's mild, yet convincing, demeanor as the choice to sooth the ire of rural zoning opponents.

"It would be an understatement to say that farmers were antagonistic and felt threatened by the new rule," Frank said. "As landowners, they had always been able to do with their property as they pleased. They felt the zoning ordinance would deny them their rights and freedoms to decide the use of their land. Some even felt the zoning plan would prohibit their sons or daughters from building homes on their own farms. That wasn't the case, of course, but I had a lot of explaining to do."

Frank's role as head of the zoning commission was to travel across the county, sometimes alone and sometimes in the company of commissioner chairman Lloyd C. Amos, to explain the new regulations and convince property owners the ordinance was designed to protect rather than harm them. "It wasn't always easy, but I never felt any particular hardship in doing it," Frank added. That, in essence, has been Frank's approach to every community project he has led.

Bain said it took a special kind of person and personality to succeed in that initial countywide zoning task. "Stanley did it and did a good job, just as Sidney and I knew he would. That's how it all got started. Sidney was Stanley's mentor. Stanley listened carefully and closely to Sidney and didn't make too many moves without Sidney's advice. Sidney wanted to get Stanley involved in civic work and wanted him to become civic minded because he knew the result would be good. Stanley is a natural leader and he has proved that when he gets into something

Stanley Frank and Gov. Terry Sanford, 1960. Sanford was one of many governors who asked Frank to serve on boards and commissions to improve economic and environmental conditions in North Carolina. Frank served Sanford as a member of the Governor's Executive Committee for Employment of the Handicapped. Frank worked with governors from Sanford (1960) through Jim Hunt (2000).

he is determined to make it work. His willingness to tackle any task is one of his greatest assets and among his finest attributes. He is a workaholic, and in his case that is not just a cliché. It's a fact."

Stern, who died in August 1991, sought the help of Bain to get Frank involved because Frank was in those years not part of the established Greensboro business community. Frank also was not considered a member of an established Greensboro family — as his brief exclusion from the Sedgefield Country Club showed — and was not in a business that was considered mainstream like, for example, the textile industry. Frank at the time was also still struggling financially with the company he purchased when it had limited customers and he had relatively few assets.

While Frank was known among close associates for his work ethic in the 1950s, he had not become a part of the city's elite inner circle of Cones, Prices, Lindleys, Sternbergers, Borens and Vanstorys. Stern wanted his friend Frank more involved because he felt Frank could succeed and prove he was as worthy as any other businessperson in town. Time has proved Stern correct.

"His only mistake is that he always does everything anyone ever asks of him," Bain said of Frank. "He never says no. He has been a definite strength in this community just as he was in his business and has been in his family."

From those early days of Sedgefield and county zoning issues, Frank moved on to the regional airport authority where he served as chairman during critical periods of development and growth. He served on a series of boards at Guilford College, Wake Forest University, and the University of North Carolina at Greensboro. He was one of the original members of the Greensboro Development Corporation, an organization of chief executive officers of local corporations. He has served on national, state and regional boards and been cited numerous times for his civic and business endeavors. His achievements, however, frequently have gone without much public recognition because that's the way he wanted it. The one thing he has never done is seek public office; he never wanted that.

While others were in the spotlight, he was in the shadows. Often as not, he was getting things done while others were talking about what ought to be done. A complete list of his accomplishments and awards may well stretch longer than his five-foot, five-inch height.

Frank undertook many of these projects while growing a small, nearly bankrupt business in Southeast Greensboro into an internationally known enterprise that generated ample resources to secure his family and bring him international recognition as a leader in his industry. His civic work and benevolence have served the community for 60-plus years and he has worked to ensure that his good works will continue well into the future. Through his own careful estate planning, Frank and his wife have created a financial structure to ensure that their assets will eventually remain for use in the local community through the Stanley and Dorothy Frank Family Foundation.

Frank's friends and those who have watched his civic involvement through the years insist his quiet record of achievement without seeking public recognition should be a role model for others to follow.

Frank is philosophical about it all. "You have to be realistic and try to evaluate what you can accomplish. But you have to believe in yourself. Greensboro has been so good to my family and me that I feel I ought to give back as much or more than I have received. But what I have accomplished hasn't been just of my own doing. Many other people are due a lot of credit."

While Frank's civic projects have been both broad and deep across the region and state, his benevolent efforts have not been limited to governmental boards and commissions or to official committees. Much of his community work has been simply assisting individuals with special needs.

Perhaps the best way to describe his help to others is to let them explain in their own words.

Shirley Frye, wife of former N.C. Supreme Court Chief Justice Henry Frye and herself a civic activist:

"Stanley has helped me develop strength and perseverance." In 1970, Frye was chosen as the first black president of the Greensboro YWCA. In her first few months in office a crisis arose after she asked for the resignation of two white staff members who had approved $25,000 in spending without prior approval from the board. The money was part of the then United Community Services (later United Way) contribution to the Y. Frank was chairman of the UCS at the time.

Not surprisingly, the issue became a racial one. Newspaper stories of the spending and resignation actions noted the racial connotations. Frye was then new to public controversy and was more than a little perplexed about how to handle the problem. She sought advice and counsel of Frank.

"He just listened and he understood the issues and my anxiety. He was the catalyst for a resolution. I felt comfortable with his handling it. He didn't pull any punches with the people or the newspaper, but he willingly stepped forward, defused the emotions, and solved the problem. He was my saving grace."

While Frye's debt of gratitude to Frank was still fresh in her mind, he came to the aid of her attorney husband, Henry, who was facing his first election campaign after being appointed chief justice of the North Carolina Supreme Court.

"Stanley asked Henry if he needed any campaign help and Henry said he couldn't answer that because of judicial campaign rules. I said, 'Well, I can answer it and, yes, he needs help.' Stanley said 'I'll take care of it.' Pretty soon the campaign contributions started coming in. He knows how to make contacts and accomplish things."

Kay Stern, widow of Frank's lawyer and friend Sidney Stern:

"Stanley never says no to anyone asking for anything. He's very kind and generous. That's his way of helping friends. He and Dorothy are major strengths in this community and their real strength lies in their character. What those two have done for and meant to this community is remarkable. They are both the salt of the earth."

The Greensboro Board of Directors for First Union National Bank, May 29, 1979. Seated (left to right) are Charles Saldarini, Kay Stern, Hargrove "Skipper" Bowles, Charles McLendon, Stanley Frank and Paul Schenck Jr. Standing are Dr. Thomas Henson, Kirby Moore, Marvin Legare, Y.C. Hines, Edward Alexander, Charles Reid, Donald Lowe, Elmer Yost, David Petty and John G.B. Ellison.

Becky Troxler, a Carolina By-Product office employee for 16 years:

"He is a most wonderful person and was a benevolent employer. He never wanted any of his workers to leave the company; if they did leave, he was interested in why, to see if something needed to be improved, to see if somehow he could help. His kindness to me and my family has been wonderful."

When Troxler's husband, Vestal, was diagnosed with pancreatic cancer, Frank gave her unlimited time off with full pay and benefits. "He gave me three months off, but basically I was in and out for a full year before my husband's death in 1983. Stanley told me that if I needed anything, just to let him know. He never once questioned my absence. Instead, he was always there for me, offering assistance. He truly cared. Even after he left the company, he told me if I ever needed another job to come see him. That's the way he is."

Angie Glascock, a Carolina By-Product secretary for 25 years:

"He was demanding and wanted things done right. But if you did your job right he was a wonderful employer. When any of his employees had a problem, he always bent over backwards to help. He was genuinely concerned of people's needs and willing to help. He was loyal to everyone."

Alice Evans, the Frank family housekeeper for more than three decades:

"If everyone could grow old the way they [Frank and his wife Dorothy] have, the world would be a wonderful place. They are really caring people. They genuinely serve their community and want to help those who want to help themselves. I would have stopped working a long time ago if they had not been such fine people. I stay on because they are so nice. I've always gotten respect from that family and he is always offering to help where there is a need."

Dr. Xaver Hertle, long-time friend:
"Stanley is one of the few real gentlemen I know. When people he knows retire, he's always asking if he can help with anything. He is simply a very good person and he is so appreciative of things. You could give him a piece of chocolate and he'll thank you as if it were a gold watch."

The late Alexander Spears, who was for many years a corporate executive and colleague on the boards of Guilford College and the local airport authority:
"I have been amazed with Stanley's amount of energy and enthusiasm for community and civic involvement. His desire to remain active and stay involved never ceases. The airport has been one of his major undertakings and he has not liked letting go of that. His contributions in time, talent and resources to the airport and to Guilford College and so many other worthy programs have been tremendous. He has been involved in so many projects for so long that he has to rank near the top of important people in this community in terms of what he has accomplished."

Richard (Dick) McCaskill, friend and golfing partner:
"I have never met a person who was a greater servant for his city and state. He is fair in all things, never bragging and never pretentious. He knows so many people and is ready to be of service to each of them if a need arises. I am confident that if I told him I had a need, he'd say 'How much and how can I help?'"
McCaskill was in the threesome on the golf

course when Frank, who has a habit of walking ahead of his golfing partners, was struck on the leg by a wayward shot off the club of Jack Dixon. "Jack, you need to work on your aim," Frank replied as he rubbed the injured leg and determined his injury wasn't serious. "He is very private and quiet, but he has a great sense of humor," McCaskill said.

Roger Soles, long-time friend and board member of the Frank Family Foundation:

"He's a hard man to turn down when he asks for something. He has been one of the more active members of the Greensboro Development Corporation, even from the earliest days when it met privately with just a few people, usually in the dining room of Burlington Industries. I admire his energy. He is enthusiastic about everything. Whatever is good for the community, he works for it."

Ted Sumner, former First Union National Bank official in Greensboro and Charlotte:

"Stanley is an excellent community representative who realizes the benefit and importance of giving back to the community. I quickly learned that he is one of the leaders in Greensboro. You could always go to him. He was not just a member, but a contributing member of the First Union Corporate Board. He made the board a part of himself. I admire him greatly."

Ralph Stout Sr., a friend for more than 60 years until his death in December 2000:

"Loyalty is Stanley's greatest attribute. His loyalty is outstanding. It's hard to dispute him because he is almost always right in assessing things. He was never very good at golf because by the fourth or fifth tee he was talking about something else. He told me one day he had five friends who owed him substantial amounts of money. He didn't have anything in writing on the loans. He just trusted the people and had helped them out. I think he got about half of his loans back, but I don't know if he ever got the other half."

(At various intervals during the decades of the 1960s and 1970s, Frank often loaned money to friends to start businesses that became viable and well-known enterprises. One example was Bi-Lo Supermarket. Frank's initial loan to that grocery chain was instrumental in the founder's getting the business started.)

In the late 1970s, on Stout's recommendation, Frank purchased a 660-acre farm in Rockingham County with 10,000 feet of frontage along the Dan River and a 130-acre tobacco allotment. Frank paid $300 an acre. He was later offered $700 an acre and then $1,000 an acre by potential buyers. He didn't want to sell the land, but didn't like to pay property taxes, so he deeded the property to his two sons, Bill and Barry.

Al Schiff, retired corporate executive who, quite literally, met Frank over a scoop of grits:
"There is an enormous amount of breadth and depth to the man. What you see, you like; and the more you see, the more you appreciate him. He just says and does the right things for the community."

Schiff's introduction to Frank was at a civic project buffet breakfast. "I passed by the grits and Stanley, whom I didn't know, was behind me in line. He asked why I passed up the grits and I told him I didn't like the taste. He reached out, put a huge spoonful on my plate, and asked that I try them. I still don't like grits, but I surely do like Stanley."

Blake Clark, former partner with Frank in the owner-

ship of the Greensboro Generals:

"He is interested in doing good for the community without broadcasting his name. He is an outstanding citizen for Greensboro and the region. I think when he came South from New York, he thought he had died and gone to heaven. He is just an ordinary golfer, but he surely has been a supportive, substantial backer of the Jaycees and the Greater Greensboro Open (GGO). He is a very loyal Green Coater [former golf tournament honorary chairman]."

Frank's love of golf and his efforts to promote the popular annual Jaycee-sponsored GGO (later the

Stanley Frank, a regular golfer for decades and patron of the Jaycee-sponsored professional golf tournament, somehow managed to rescue his errant ball from behind a tree at Sedgefield Country Club during the 1974 pro-am day.

Greater Greensboro Chrysler Classic) have been among his most active and enjoyable volunteer civic efforts over several decades. Year after year, Frank used his company plane without charge to ferry golfers and entertainers to the tournament or to fly Jaycees or business leaders to other golf tournaments to recruit golfers for the GGO.

Frank did, however, get a few perks for his services; he got to play golf with some of the better professionals and many of the big-name entertainers on the pro-am days of tournament week. He was paired with Arnold Palmer and Pat Boone on one pro-am day, remembered as much for tragedy as for golf, and once spent the day playing with Perry Como on a day that caused more than a few anxious moments for Jaycees.

At the 1968 GGO pro-am, Frank was teamed with Palmer and Boone. That was the week Martin Luther King, Jr. was killed. "It was a rewarding experience to play with those two even though it was a lousy, cold and rainy day," Frank explained. "But the most vivid and disturbing recollection of that tournament was the death of King. The Sunday finals were postponed until the next day in King's memory. Billy Casper won in the rain."

The day he spent with Como was perfectly clear and sunny. That is what caused the anxiety among Jaycees and Frank's family. Frank flew his company airplane from Greensboro to Florida to pick up the entertainer, who was to perform in Greensboro that night at the pro-am banquet. But Como didn't want to come directly to Greensboro. He asked Frank to stop in Pinehurst so the two could play golf at the Country Club of North Carolina. Frank, trying to hide his sheer delight at the suggestion, said, well, he guessed that would be all right.

"We played 18 holes," Frank said, "and then he

wanted to play nine more. I told him it might make us late for the banquet."

"So, what are they going to do, start without me?" Como asked with a grin.

They played another nine holes, then flew to Greensboro barely in time for Como to perform. "I seem to recall that Dorothy wasn't too happy with me, and I think some of the Jaycees were a little worried. But everything worked out just fine." What Frank recalls most vividly is the day of fun.

The GGO tournament also once caused Frank and his family more than a little anguish, the singular blemish on an otherwise long and fruitful relationship with the Greensboro Jaycees, although he has never been a member of the club. His home was robbed during a golf tournament function.

Jaycee officials during one tournament dismissed a club member and banned him from involvement in future tournament activities after he was accused of stealing concession receipts. During a later tournament, on the night of the well-publicized pro-am banquet, the Frank home was robbed and the house was ransacked. All the family silver, cherished since the Frank marriage, was stolen. A year later, the Jaycee who had been accused of making off with concession money was charged with the break-in and robbery. "It was a sizeable loss of property, but more significantly, we felt violated, having a stranger go through our home that way. That was not a pleasant experience," Frank said of the nighttime robbery. He never learned if his house was chosen by the robber who knew Frank and his wife would be at a GGO event, but said that was likely the case.

The home robbery aside, Frank said he had only fond memories of his many productive decades of community service since his initial involvement in civic

Stanley Frank (center) and Wake Forest alumnus Charles Reid during a discussion with former President Gerald Ford at a Wake Forest University conference in May, 1980.

projects.

"It is something I wanted to do, something that needed to be done and the kind of thing that I hope others will do," Frank said of his community work. "This is a wonderful community with wonderful people. I am glad I made this my home and became a part of the many good things that have happened here. The only regret is that there comes a time when you just have to step aside and let someone else take the lead. For me, that is hard to do, but I understand the reasons."

Another thing that was hard for Frank was the decision to sell his company. He might not have, he said, except for worrisome federal government interference. The meddlesome government involvement in the matter proved to Frank and his family how a seemingly uncaring bureaucracy could harm productive businesses and stymie economic growth and development.

Frank isn't bitter about the circumstances surrounding the company sale, but he is still agitated about the heavy hand of the Internal Revenue Service that convinced him it would be best to take action that he really didn't want to take. It is a classic case in which a businessman was doing nothing wrong — in fact, quite the contrary. But government bureaucrats, who wouldn't listen to what Frank feels was reason and common sense explanations, stifled rather than encouraged private enterprise. How all that came about is one of the many interesting, albeit then and now troubling, aspects of his productive business and civic life.

The government altered Frank's business. But it didn't slow him down. He just changed his focus on his business, while keeping up with his civic projects.

11

Tax Headaches & Sales Heartaches

Business was running so smoothly for Stanley Frank and Carolina By-Products in the first decade that he owned the company, he privately wondered how long the good news could and would last. He found out from an unlikely, unexpected and unbending source: the Internal Revenue Service.

The IRS action was not a pleasant experience, and it brought levels of anxiety he had not encountered since his earliest days in town when company profits were few and problems were many. It was the IRS demands that ultimately convinced Frank that single stockholder ownership of a successful and profitable enterprise was not in the best interest of him or his family and brought on his decision to sell the company.

The history of the company under prior owners, of course, had not been glowing. Carolina By-Products was on the verge of financial collapse when the two owners — one in Washington and one in Norfolk—

sent 21-year-old Frank to Greensboro in early 1936. His initial laborer's duties included collecting by-products from meat markets and packinghouses and kitchen grease from restaurants to begin the process of converting the raw materials into usable consumer products.

Starting with one dilapidated Dodge truck and a handful of unskilled coworkers, Frank began carrying out his role by increasing efficiency, adding suppliers and expanding production. After Frank was named plant manager just four months after coming to town, profits steadily increased each year over the next decade when, shockingly, in 1953, both company owners died just days apart.

Frank thought of leaving the company after the deaths of the dual owners. His wife Dorothy urged him to do just that. "She thought I ought to get into something else," he said. "We didn't know if the company could make it," Frank said. That's one of the few times in his 60-plus years of marriage and corporate leadership that Frank ignored his wife's recommendations. "I just didn't listen to her that time," he said. His choice turned out to be the right one.

Rather than leave, Frank took a major gamble and did something he had never done before and hasn't done since. He went heavily into debt and bought the company. Having first worked there and then managed the company for absentee owners, he saw the potential and felt comfortable that if he had total control he could make things significantly better. He didn't, he said, want to walk away and see the company fall into strange or uncaring hands.

During the middle and late 1950s with Frank as owner and in total command of business decisions, profits climbed even higher. He emphasized efficient production and customer service. Working always six and sometimes seven days a week, he insisted on a careful accounting of every aspect of the production and marketing process. He personally checked on missed collections of restaurant kitchen grease. He monitored quality of tallow and animal feed products. He insisted on reduction of olfactory emissions and kept tabs on bookkeeping details. He worked diligently to add value to everything the company was doing.

Reluctantly, although out of what he considered necessity, Frank borrowed approximately $1 million to buy Carolina By-Products, a staggering figure for him at the time, and he was determined to see his risk show rewards. Detesting the debt, he managed the company frugally and turned virtually all profits into paying off his loan and saving for future growth in his first years as owner.

During those years in the rendering business, Frank established a reputation for quality products and visionary thinking. His involvement with a division of Eastman Kodak illustrates the point.

Between 1953 and 1955, officials at Tennessee Eastman, a division of the giant photographic company, asked Frank and Carolina By-Products to help devise an improved method of stabilizing inedible fats to be used in manufacturing animal feed. Tennessee Eastman sought out Frank's guidance and advice, rather than that of executives of much larger chemical companies, on the belief that Frank's service would be more efficient and of higher quality. Carolina By-Product officials helped the Eastman company produce an improved antioxidant to help stabilize the inedible fats, which improved their rendering industry products and increased marketing and profits.

"It was prestigious for us that they chose our company," Frank said of the Eastman Corporation. "And it put them ahead of competitors in marketing. Their purpose was to improve their products and we feel we helped them do that."

The specialty work with Eastman Kodak was one of several steps Frank took that brought him personal and financial success. By the early 1960s his debt incurred in purchasing the company was virtually eliminated. He had also by that time repurchased the minority shares of his two Washington associates, lawyer Louis Denit and accountant J. H. Verkouteren, and he had substantial funds set aside for manufacturing expansion as well as a kind of self-insurance in case of emergencies. Flash fires, chemical explosions and other safety hazards were common in the rendering processes; Frank wanted his own financial cushion, in addition to insurance proceeds, to cover those expenses, should they occur, in order to avoid encountering more debt.

That's when the heavy hand of the federal taxman began to ensnarl him. The federal government did not approve of his method of reinvesting and saving. Their intervention Frank called harassing and bureaucratic. It took him more than 10 years and more than half a million dollars to get out of what he still feels was the unjustified vise grip of the Internal Revenue Service.

Frank was ultimately proved right in his tax fight. But even in winning that legal war, he emerged financially harmed. The tax battles were among the issues that encouraged him to sell his company.

"I was tired of the hassle and tired of fighting with the government," Frank said of his decision to sell rather than continue his decade-long fight with the tax agents.

"Oh yes, the battle with the IRS had a direct influence over my decision to sell. I began evaluating my own health and thinking of the future of my family. Those were more important to me than continued fighting with the federal bureaucrats who kept badgering me. When it was all over, I am proud to say they (IRS) admitted I had done nothing wrong. They said I had been right all along, just as I had been contending all along. I won, but they essentially drove me out of the ownership."

Frank's serious tax problems began in the early 1960s, several years before he tried without success to turn Carolina By-Products into a public corporation. He sought public shareholder interest for two reasons. First, he wanted the IRS off his back over what the government called "unreasonable accumulation of earnings" because of his sole ownership. Second, he felt that outside shareholder revenue would allow for even faster company expansion, one of his goals.

The plan to sell shares in Carolina By-Products to outside investors, however, never got beyond the talking stage or the desks of lawyers and accountants. Public interest didn't meet expectations. The rendering industry's perceived reputation as an environmentally unfriendly or unsafe enterprise dampened interest among potential shareholders.

"The plan to secure outside shareholders just didn't work out," Frank said. "Interest wasn't there and so we just had to keep dealing with the IRS and their interpretations of their rules. I was the sole owner, and the IRS didn't like that from a profit angle. I paid all the taxes due, but the government kept hounding me for more beyond my income and corporate taxes. They kept questioning what they called the undistributed earnings under section 531 of the tax code.

"I kept explaining to the tax agents that the money wasn't going to me and that we were saving the earnings to expand in the future and to protect ourselves against safety hazards, but they wouldn't listen. They wanted me to take the earnings out and pay dividends to stockholders. Well, I was the only stockholder at the time. What they wanted was for me to pay myself dividends so they could then tax me for that income in addition to the corporate and individual income tax I was already paying. I felt that was double taxation and was unfair. I wasn't getting the dividends for myself and didn't want them. I was setting aside reserve resources for future needs for the company. They said I was holding back money just for myself, which wasn't true. They claimed that I owed taxes on this money that I wasn't receiving, that I was saving so I could avoid more debt. Trying to reason with them didn't do any good.

"I showed them in our records that the company was planning to expand, to start a chemical division. We needed to have money to protect against fires or other hazards so I wouldn't have to borrow again in case of emergency. We were putting the surplus back into the company, not squandering it away. We had written our corporate minutes in a very precise manner, explaining our expansion plans, producing ample evidence. We further explained that our business was subject to major hazard expenses and that outside suppliers, for the most part, were the ones who controlled our industry. We were different from most industries because suppliers determined our destiny. We clearly demonstrated all those factors in our records and in our conversations, but the tax people wouldn't see it our way. The IRS wouldn't even consider any of that. They wouldn't listen to reason. They read our records and ignored them. They thought it was all window dressing in spite of ample evidence to the contrary."

In addition to what Frank and his advisers felt was owed, the IRS was demanding more than $400,000 in taxes from 1959 through the middle 1960s. Frank and his legal team and accountants appealed to the higher IRS officials, showing them actual construction plans for the chemical division development.

That step, after months of wrangling, got the attention of one IRS examiner who agreed to make one concession. The tax examiner, after personally reviewing the chemical division construction plans as well as a scale model of the proposed plant, agreed to defer temporarily — but not withdraw — the demand for the additional taxes.

"It was as if they didn't really trust that we were going to build the chemical division even after we showed them our plans. But they did agree to put the issue on hold while we built our new chemical plant. We did that, finished construction and put the chemical division into operation. They then came back around after the plant was finished and went through the same ritual for the next several years. The chemical plant was there. They were standing inside it. It was operational. But they continued saying we owed more taxes because we were not distributing earnings to stockholders, who, of course, did not exist. The earnings had been put in the building, not in my pocket."

At that point, Frank and his corporate lawyers decreed enough was enough. He filed suit against the

IRS, meaning he was required to place the $400,000-plus that the government said he owed in corporate taxes into an escrow account under the control of the courts until the case was resolved.

That legal action, in fact, was one of two battles Frank had with the federal tax agents during the decade of the 1960s. In a separate incident, although Frank says in all likelihood linked to the chemical division tax issue, federal agents also questioned the use of Frank's home office. He had been using one room at his Sedgefield home for business purposes and claimed a tax credit for its use. The feds frowned on that, suggesting he wasn't really working at home despite evidence to the contrary.

"They were what I'd call picayunish about everything," he said. "I was working seven days a week, bringing work home. They even had the audacity to come into my home to look at my desk, calculator and typewriter. They were snooping around, almost like the Gestapo. We had had enough and decided to bring the whole thing to a head. We filed a civil suit against the IRS."

Frank and his legal advisers, however, concluded that their best chances of winning against the government were not in tax court where they felt judges tended to favor the tax collectors. Instead, Frank brought his legal action in federal court and built his case there before Middle District Federal Judge Edwin M. Stanley, a tough but fair jurist. "The IRS didn't like it, of course, that we didn't go to tax court, but we wanted a fair hearing." The suit against the IRS was filed in 1964, four years after the IRS demands began.

Trial preparation, including depositions from Frank and his company officials as well as a series of

federal agents and high-ranking IRS officials, consumed years of time and significant dollars. Among
the government representatives required to give testimony was William D. Ruckelshaus. Ruckelshaus, at
the time with the IRS, would later become national
director of the Environmental Protection Agency and
a President Nixon administration justice department
deputy U.S. Attorney General who resigned rather than
carry out some Nixon directives pertaining to the
Watergate scandal.

In June 1971, before a jury could hear any evidence, the IRS finally conceded what Frank had contended all along. The government, the IRS said, didn't
have a case and he didn't owe the taxes. The government told him he could close his escrow account and
the money was his.

"I got great satisfaction out of that," Frank said.
"They said I was right, but offered no apologies for
the way I had been treated all those years. I felt from
the beginning that I was right. I won the fight, but it
was hard and long. The government showed how difficult it could be for business people who are trying to
do the honest and right thing. The government rules
can be unrealistic and the bureaucracy can be unreasonable. That was certainly the case with me."

Frank's satisfaction, however, was personal
rather than financial. "I ended up with nothing from
the escrow money," he said. "The lawyers and accountants wound up getting it all after their years of work.
I don't resent what they were due because they represented me well. But I do resent the way the government treated me throughout the whole ordeal. Basically, I felt then and now that I was harassed."

Frank actually sold his company in the midst of

the IRS case, five years after the suit was filed but two years before it was resolved. Part of the sales contract stipulated that if Frank won his tax case, any escrow revenue would go to him rather than the new owners. That became a moot point, when the legal and accounting bills came due and soaked up all the surplus revenue.

Frank's sale of his company was finalized March 26, 1969, to a publicly held, nationwide conglomerate operating under the name of Kane-Miller Corporation, based in New York City. The new owners controlled one other rendering plant, but their primary business at the time was investing in diversified manufacturing companies.

Kane-Miller was one of several corporate suitors who were interested in buying Carolina By-Products, despite the pending tax case. Interested buyers said they saw the success of what Frank had built.

Before Kane-Miller offered their best price, Frank negotiated with Wilson & Company, a meatpacking corporation that also was into sports equipment, and with W. R. Grace, a well-respected international manufacturing and investment company. Frank sold to Kane-Miller partly because that corporation offered the highest bid, but also because the new owners allowed Frank to continue the independent operation of Carolina By-Products.

At the time of the sale, Kane-Miller was the parent company of numerous enterprises operating in such diverse businesses as wholesale food distribution, national restaurant chains, meatpacking, vegetable oil and margarine production, poultry processing and feed ingredient manufacturing, and canning and prepared salads for delicatessens and up-scale restaurants.

Frank explained at the time of the sale that he anticipated the new owners would strengthen Carolina By-Products through increased benefits and protection via diversification. "Under no circumstances would I have considered [the sale] had I thought that the security of any of us would be threatened," he wrote employees when the sale was completed. "I have great faith in the sincerity, integrity and business acumen of our new owners."

Frank's faith in Kane-Miller was correct in 1969, and lasted for 16 years until 1985, when Kane-Miller began to change its business philosophy and started to look for other buyers. Subsequent owners didn't live up to Frank's expectations, and he eventually left the company.

Frank received $10 million for his company from Kane-Miller, a ten-fold increase from his purchase price 16 years earlier. The IRS got its share off the top; taxes on the sale totaled approximately $3 million.

The sale price was covered three ways. Of the total $10 million, Frank and his sons, who were then part owners, received $8 million in cash. Frank accepted a promissory note from the new owners of $1 million, to be repaid in two equal payments, and accepted another $1 million in Kane-Miller stock.

Even though extremely profitable for Frank and his family, the sale of the company was clearly not an action that brought much joy to his household because it was brought on by the tax problems, all unfounded and unfair in his view. Frank then and later felt the IRS penalized him for his business success solely because he didn't have stockholders outside his family.

The trauma of the sale, however, could be termed mild compared to later events at Carolina By-Products that began in 1985. A series of subsequent sales and revolving door owners ultimately meant that Frank, his two sons and other top company officials would all leave. Frank retired in early 1988. Oldest son Bill was fired shortly afterwards and youngest son Barry resigned, all within the first months of 1988.

That left the Franks worried and wondering what might happen to the enterprise they had worked so hard to build. Regrettably, some of their worst fears turned into reality in the decade after they severed their ties with company operations.

Frank had given each of his two sons 22.5 percent of the company ownership in 1965 during the middle of the IRS harangue. Because of their relatively young ages —Bill was 24 and Barry 20 — Frank put their shares in a trust. That decision had no impact on the tax controversy.

Frank and his sons were the sole stockholders in Carolina By-Products until the chemical division, Chemol, was opened in the midst of the IRS battle. Frank offered three other company officials — Chemol president Len Anderson, Carolina By-Products president Fred Schuster, and sales manager Tom McNulty — the opportunity to own stock in the chemical division. Frank later repurchased their shares before he sold the company to Kane-Miller.

Earlier, in the late 1950s, Frank had initiated a profit-sharing plan for company employees. He did that before most Southern companies had such programs and certainly much sooner than most small companies began similar practices. Any employee with 30 months employment was eligible for a percentage of the profits each year. "I did that because I always wished I had had that kind of opportunity when I was younger. I felt the dedicated workers ought to be able to enjoy company earnings that they had helped generate. Profit sharing was beneficial to employees and was great at promoting company loyalty."

Frank labeled his profit-sharing program the three Ps, representing what he called "people, pride, and performance" in the Preferred Payment Plan.

In addition to the early profit-sharing plan, the opening of Chemol is one of the many innovative aspects of the way Frank ran his company. He was thinking outside the box long before that term became fashionable with management gurus, many of whom have made careers out of telling corporate owners how to reinvent their companies through the teamwork concept.

Frank formed his own successful team without the involvement of high-priced management consultants. He used what turned out to be good judgment even as he took risks at trying new ways of better using his employees and his company facilities. He didn't have to serve demands of outside stockholders or whims of consultants. He just did it his way, which proved successful.

The initial concept for what became Chemol was started six years before the chemical division opened in 1965. Frank hired a mild-mannered but enthusiastic ex-Marine named Leonard (Len) W. Anderson, who held degrees from Yale University and Harvard Business School. That hire came about through a recommendation from Frank's lawyer and friend Sidney Stern Jr., the same man who put Frank on the road toward civic work in the Greensboro community.

Anderson, fresh from the business school classroom at Harvard following his Yale undergraduate studies and military experience, took to heart the advice of a favorite professor when he agreed to the job offer from Frank. The advice, which most of Anderson's classmates looking for prestigious corporate ladders ignored, was to look for a small company where he could make a difference. That, the professor said, would make life more meaningful.

Anderson had married a member of the Stern family and had learned of Carolina By-Products through the family connection. "Sidney asked me to consider going to work for the company. I didn't know anything about the rendering industry and wasn't too interested at first, but Sidney sent me a few financial statements," Anderson said. "They looked pretty impressive. I saw the potential. I remembered the words of my professor and decided to take a chance with this small outfit in the South."

Anderson joined Carolina By-Products in 1958 at $125 a week.

"My first day on the job Stanley asked me what I wanted to do," Anderson said. "I told him I didn't know."

"Well, you may as well learn from the ground up," Frank responded. The first assignment: driving a truck and picking up kitchen grease from restaurants and inedible animal by-products from butcher shops.

Anderson was the first college graduate ever hired at Carolina By-Products. "And I'm pretty sure that I was the first Yale and Harvard Business School graduate who ever rode in a smelly truck and picked up grease and inedible animal parts," Anderson said of his initial duties. He spent six months on the truck routes.

But there were much brighter days ahead.

"Stanley was always looking for good people," Anderson said. "He often said to me that if he could find a good, ambitious and dedicated employee, that person would never cost the company a dime and he could not pay that person enough because they would contribute much more to the company than they could earn in salary. He always had that attitude. I think he was right, too."

Frank apparently saw in Anderson, a man with a soft voice and appealing personality, the image of the employee role model he described. Anderson was one of two young men hired by Frank at the end of the 1950s and early 1960s to fit that mold. The other was Steve Wilkerson, at the time a Greensboro stockbroker who, like Anderson, made the company connection through a family friend.

Wilkerson's connection was Winston-Salem oil company owner and Democratic Party powerbroker Bert Bennett. "I was looking for something different from dealing with unseen clients by phone, so Bert put me in touch with Skipper Bowles, who he said knew everything about the business world in Greensboro," Wilkerson said. "Skipper and Stanley Frank were close friends and that's how the connection was made." Bennett, Bowles and Frank were all members of the board of First Union National Bank in Charlotte. Bowles would later be the state's Democratic Party nominee for governor. His son, Erskine, served during the 1990s as chief of staff for President Bill Clinton.

While Anderson was taking a leadership role in the new chemical division, Wilkerson was serving as a procurement manager of the Gastonia facilities and later became the facilities general manager and senior vice president.

Frank had been privately contemplating the creation of the chemical division for some time in the early 1960s because he felt it would be a worthwhile and profitable aspect of the company. He had begun putting away funds for the division's creation when the IRS agents began their bothersome invasion of the company's finances.

"Stanley came to me one day and said he was considering starting the chemical process part of the company," Anderson said. "He wanted to put profits back into the company. He felt we could make useful chemical products from animal fats we produced and asked me to look into it. I didn't know anything about chemistry. He had a lot of faith in me, I guess. But he was taking a big chance and we were up to our ears in a risky venture for a while. His initial investment was about $250,000, but he had been saving up company profits for this purpose."

Through trial and error Anderson took the lead in learning the process of turning animal fats into additional uses. Frank was monitoring the progress each step of the way.

Carolina By-Products, of course, had been routinely turning out tallow from animal fats as part of the normal rendering process. Frank wanted broader and better uses for the tallow. Anderson and Frank learned to produce additional derivatives from animal fats through a hydrogenation process that transformed the soft fats into a white hardened tallow that, after flaking, was sold to textile companies that used the material in yarn manufacturing.

"He wanted an outlet for every pound of tallow produced," Anderson said of his mentor Frank. "He felt the market was there for the chemical process that would be beneficial for the textile industry and he wanted to be a part of it. He is an innovator and took the lead in wanting his industry to invest in new ideas and products. I admire the way he ran his company and the way he serves his community. He was demanding of his employees, but also was fair and showed compassion and concern for them. I learned a lot from him and have tried to absorb his ideas and his habits."

Chemol, Anderson said, was a "mildly profitable" division of Carolina By-Products before Frank sold the company. More importantly, however, was the fact that Frank worked to create the new division as an additional outlet for surplus tallow as well as a hedge against future lower commodity markets. This is the same course he later followed when a sizable part of his marketing included exports to parts of Europe and Asia, thanks in large part to Frank's personal trips to foreign lands to expand his market. He traveled extensively over Europe, Asia and Africa to promote both his products at Carolina By-Products and the rendering industry nationwide as president of the National Renderers Association. He also brought Japanese and other foreign businessmen to his Greensboro plant to enhance their knowledge and use of more modern by-product manufacturing processes.

In 1965, he was one of two United States businessmen from the rendering industry who traveled to Africa to help teach ways to improve sanitation methods through wider use of soap and other cleansing agents produced by the rendering industry.

"Believe it or not," Frank said in making that trip, "but there are a lot of people in parts of the world who don't know what soap is." On that trip, Frank helped teach Africans how to manufacture soap and offered technical advice on ways to improve the country's feed industry.

There was no part of production, as the African trip showed, that Frank left untapped if it meant more efficient and broader marketing.

Frank's interest in Chemol was not unlike his interest in other phases of the company operations. He maintained a watchful eye — literally — on the animal fat extraction process just as he did on chemical processes and financial stability. He located his office desk — after adding an office window for a better view — so he could observe route collections of by-products being unloaded for processing.

And just to make sure he didn't miss anything, Frank installed a mirror on the back wall behind his desk so when he turned around to take phone calls he could still watch the production process from the unloading platforms. He didn't do that to spy on employees, he said, but rather to help ensure continuous efficiency of production. Carolina By-Products had a small management team and each member was assigned specific monitoring duties.

He didn't cut workers much slack if he felt they were not producing at a high level. "He could rake employees over the coals when they deserved it, but he was really pretty soft-hearted," Anderson said. "He could be tough at times, but he was always looking for ways to help people. He sometimes seemed more generous with his workers than with himself. He never asked his employees to do anything he was not willing to do."

Frank's warm feelings toward employees extended beyond their working years, too. He encouraged them to return to the company for visits and conversation, but few ever did.

"He wondered why former employees never came back to see him," Anderson said. "He was really soft-hearted and cared for them. They all admired and respected him greatly, but I think most were a little intimidated to just go in his office and chat. His reputation was such that it would be a little like an enlisted man going to visit General Patton. It just didn't happen very often."

Wilkerson, who remained with the company much longer than Frank and his sons or Anderson, offered a similar assessment of the way the company ran under Frank's ownership.

"He was like a general," Wilkerson said. "He held the proverbial corner office. He could be tough, but he cared about employees and worked hard to ensure their happiness and longevity with the company. Some workers who probably should have been fired were retained because Stanley personally cared about them and their families. He handled the business like a father handling his children. Discipline was sometimes needed, but care and concern were always present. He and company president Fred Schuster performed in such a way that people wanted to do the right thing. They salvaged people. We had a source of pride in those days when he owned the company. That kind of care is not duplicated today. Once he left the company, it was never quite like home again."

Schuster and Frank worked closely in running the company and became best personal friends. Carolina By-Products was once a client of Schuster's when he was an area sales manager for International Harvester and supplied Carolina By-Products with trucks.

He and Frank held mutual respect after working with each other for several years, and Frank hired him to help run the company. Schuster became president in 1970 when Frank became board chairman.

But it was not just Frank's employees who offered praise. Even competitors agreed on the efficiency of the way the company was run under Frank's leadership. "He is a wise old gentleman, a shrewd businessman who earned the respect of all those he encountered," said Dennis Griffin, owner of a competing family-run rendering company with plants in 14 states stretching from the east coast to the middle west. "I've known Stanley Frank for 40 years and he has always been a leader in our industry. He always looked at the big picture, worked with intensity, always with good values and high moral character. He cared for his employees."

Among the benefits Frank extended to his hourly workers was free health insurance each December. He never deducted the employee cost of health coverage in December in order to provide extra take-home pay for employees during the holiday season. He also paid for tickets to motor sports events at Charlotte Motor Speedway for his workers who were auto race fans.

Carolina By-Products files are filled with memos from Frank to his employees thanking them for their performance during the time he owned the company and after the sale while he remained as president. As prices of the manufactured products slipped during the middle 1980s, Frank's volume of memos expressing his appreciation for job performance increased.

Prices in the summer of June 1986 dropped to their lowest level in more than a decade, but Frank thanked his employees for their continued good efforts at production in the face of sluggish markets, both domestic and foreign. "Our diversity of products has helped us fare better than most," Frank wrote in a memo to his loyal workers. "We will have a narrow profit margin and a low return on investment, but through astute, aggressive and diversified manufacturing and marketing, we will be able to continue with capital improvements and research and development."

Anderson said Frank applied the same rules to his two sons, who worked at Carolina By-Products, as he did to other employees. "He expected a lot of both sons. He expected them to produce. They were considered a regular part of the workforce." The jobs of the sons were secure, of course, as long as they wanted to work at the company, but their dad never insisted that they remain in his employ. Neither son flaunted his relationship to the company owner. Their dad wouldn't allow it nor would they have wanted to do it.

From early ages, well before Frank gave them a share of the ownership, both sons chose to work for Carolina By-Products where they remained through the company sale and until their unpleasant departures dictated by new owners in 1988.

•

Bill Frank, born October 1, 1941, never worked anywhere else from his teen years until new owners abruptly fired him in early 1988. He held various duties, at company plants in both Greensboro and Gastonia, and was vice president of fleet operations in his last assignment. Barry Frank also worked both at the Greensboro and Gastonia plants and was vice president of material procurement when he left the company, shortly after his brother was fired and his father retired. Neither son ever reported directly to his father in his job, instead working for other company officials.

Beginning in 1958, Bill Frank worked at Carolina By-Products during the summers of his high school years for 25 cents an hour. He framed his first fulltime weekly paycheck of $22.63. He graduated from Oak Ridge Military Academy in 1960 and enrolled at St. Andrews Presbyterian College in Laurinburg, North Carolina, but withdrew in his junior year, swapping the academic classroom for on the job training at his father's company.

Like other employees, Bill Frank's first duties included learning truck routes and picking up animal by-products and kitchen grease from meat markets and restaurants. He continued that assignment for two years before his father transferred him to the company plant in Gastonia, where his initial salary was $87.50, even though by that time a minority ownership share in the company was held for him in trust. While in Gastonia, he joined the National Guard even though he was not particularly fond of the military and likely would have been exempt for health reasons.

Bill Frank had been warned by his doctor never to join the military because of his childhood polio. That fact brought him no relief from Guilford Draft Board personnel. A female official in the High Point Selective Service office, where Frank had registered in 1964, had made it known, according to his mother that, "the Frank boy was to be drafted," regardless of a doctor's directive. Frank joined the National Guard, he said, to escape the hassle of a selective service battle over his health problems and also to lessen his chances of battle in Vietnam.

Bill Frank worked in Gastonia for five years before being asked by his father to return to Greensboro to take over supervision of the company truck fleet, consisting of some 400 units. By that time, the senior Frank had sold Carolina By-Products but was still managing the company. "He knew the trucking side of our business from top to bottom," Frank said of his oldest son, "and he was good at it."

Shortly after his return to Greensboro from Gastonia in the fall of 1969, Bill Frank accepted a friend's invitation to a party that rather quickly brought a major change in his life as a bachelor. At the party, he met an Aycock Junior High School math teacher named Hughlene Bostian, who had come to Greensboro from her native Rowan County by way of Appalachian State University. She was in personality Bill Frank's opposite. He was, then and now, introverted, soft-spoken and circumspect in words and action. She was, then and now, sprightly, outgoing and buoyant with intense views readily expressed.

It was a case of opposites attracting, immediately and lasting. "She was just so dynamic, even the way she talked," Frank said of his initial introduction to the teacher who would shortly thereafter become his wife. "In fact, I asked her out on a date the next night. Our relationship just sort of fell into place. This was in late August and we knew by Thanksgiving that we wanted to be married." The couple became engaged on New Year's Eve of 1970 and married on June 21 of the same year.

The wedding was held at Greensboro's Temple Emanuel, where Frank's parents were married. Shortly before the marriage, Hughlene Frank converted from her Protestant upbringing in the Lutheran church to Judaism in an effort to help blend herself into the close

Frank family relationship. The marriage has lasted, but her Judaism didn't. "I felt at the time like I was wearing the wrong size shoes," she said. "It [Judaism] just didn't fit. It wasn't right for me then. But as I have matured, I've come to accept the Jewish view as the real foundation of the Christian view of life. I don't see it as foreign any more and I have become more comfortable with that faith." Bill Frank has maintained his allegiance to the Jewish faith, but his wife has returned to the Lutheran church even though she still regularly participates in Jewish Holy Days with the Frank family. They have no children.

After leaving Carolina By-Products, Bill Frank worked for two years for Combustion System Sales, an industrial boiler company, and for five years as a parts supervisor for the N. C. Department of Transportation. He was unemployed from 1995 until early 2000, when he began work as a consultant for US Packaging Company in Greensboro. His job involves cost control on leased tractor-trailers.

He serves on the Guilford College Board of Visitors, as does his wife, and on the board of trustees at the Greensboro Historical Museum. He is a member of the Greensboro Sports Council, following in his father's footsteps, and the Greensboro Rotary Club. He maintains a quiet and conservative lifestyle. His hobbies include physical workouts, "although it doesn't show," and golf, "which I play poorly," he added.

Barry Frank, born September 12, 1945, began his duties at Carolina By-Products much like his older brother. His first assignment from his father was as an assistant on the truck routes. Barry's transformation to full-time employment, however, was markedly different from his sibling's.

Barry spent one year of middle school at Oak Ridge Military Academy, following his older brother there, but was pulled out by his parents. "My grades there were so good that mom and dad said something must be wrong and they were convinced I wasn't getting a very good education," Barry Frank said. He enrolled at private Darlington School in Rome, Georgia, for two years, then returned home and graduated in 1963 at age 17 with the first class from Grimsley High School, formerly Greensboro Senior High.

Then came a year at Bolles School, a college preparatory institution in Jacksonville, Florida. He also attended Chipola Junior College in Marianna, Florida, and Guilford College in Greensboro.

After his stints at the various schools during the turbulent 1960s, Barry returned home to join the family business, first working on truck routes and later handling marketing and distribution of the corporation's products. But he still wanted to prove to himself that he could handle the academic rigors of college and tried college a third time.

He proved he could do the academic work, but his heart was still with his father's company. He left the classroom for good without a degree. "I did very well academically when I tried college the final time, but I was like a fish out of water," he said in his outgoing and direct style of communication, the opposite of his older sibling. "I wanted to work, so I came home again, this time to stay." He planned to return to Carolina By-Products offices in Greensboro.

By that time, in the fall of 1969, however, the senior Frank had another assignment for his second son. "Much to my dislike," Barry said, "Dad transferred me to the company's Gastonia facility, where I was asked to learn different aspects of the business. Although I wasn't excited about the assignment at the time, it was a good learning experience and one that I learned to enjoy thoroughly. I am glad I had the opportunity."

Four years later, Barry Frank was brought back to Greensboro where he became a company vice president with responsibility for material procurement at company plants in Greensboro, Gastonia, Fayetteville, Asheville and Knoxville, Tennessee. He held that job until he resigned in early 1988.

In 1975, Barry Frank married Sharon Lewis, of Ormond Beach, Florida. The marriage was short-lived.

In 1985, Barry married Carol Ham Robinson, of Greensboro, a divorcee with two young daughters, Katie and Kelly. That marriage lasted 10 years, ending in 1995, without producing any Frank grandchildren. During the marriage and since the divorce, Barry Frank has served as a second father to the girls and provided, among other things, their primary support to attend Greensboro Day School and assistance for college expenses.

By the fall of 2000, Katie Robinson had earned a degree from Meredith College, completed studies at Wake Forest Medical School to become a physician's assistant and had married. Kelly Robinson earned a soccer scholarship to Florida State University in 1999, but heel and knee injuries cut short her sports career. In the fall of 2000 she began her sophomore year at University of North Carolina at Chapel Hill.

Since leaving Carolina By-Products, Barry Frank has run his own consulting company, National Proteins and Oils, Inc., out of an office in downtown Greensboro, just down the hall from where his father has an office to handle financial and civic matters. He works with poultry companies and with rendering facilities, doing much of the same kind of work he did at Carolina By-Products.

Barry Frank is a boat enthusiast and a sports and vintage car devotee.

Barry Frank, like his brother, is a member of the Guilford College Board of Visitors and has been an active representative of the Wake Forest Medical School, particularly with emphasis on epilepsy. He also is a board member of the Epilepsy Institute of North Carolina.

•

From the time Stanley Frank bought Carolina By-Products in 1953, until he left in the spring of 1988, he worked diligently to expand production, improve efficiency and enhance profits through innovation. Between selling the company in 1969 and his resignation in early 1988, Frank had responsibility for managing an increasing number of facilities for the new company owners. He not only was responsible for all facilities he had originally owned in cities of the two Carolinas, but also was president of Kane-Miller's food ecology group plants in San Diego, Los Angeles and three other California cities, and one in Reno, Nevada.

As an owner and later chief executive officer for the Kane-Miller food ecology group, Frank worked toward and earned a nationwide reputation among rendering company owners for his interest and leadership in promoting enhanced environmental advancements and regulations. "Stanley spent a lot of time, effort and money on ways to improve air quality and reduce odors, unlike some in the industry," said David

Rosenstein, once Frank's chief finance officer and later, under subsequent owners, a company raw materials administrator. Rosenstein worked with Frank for 12 years before the company was sold to Kane-Miller; he is still employed by current owners.

"He would spend money to prevent problems rather than waiting for them to happen and then spending needless money fixing them," Rosenstein said of Frank. "He was a builder, an individual leader on environmental issues within the industry and Carolina By-Products under his ownership and had earned a reputation as a leader in the industry."

Deservedly proud of his accomplishments as company owner and of his growing reputation as a leader through various national rendering industry offices, Frank was reluctant to seek a buyer in 1969. That decision was a troubling one for various reasons.

The IRS problem that wouldn't seem to go away clearly bothered him. Frank's concern for the future of his sons played a role in his decision, as did his own health.

"I had encountered some health problems. I had put everything I had into the company. Dorothy and I agreed that for the sake of all of the family it would be best to sell. The decision was hard, but I think it was the right decision. It might not have been correct at the time just for the boys (Bill and Barry), but it was the right one for the whole family. Dorothy has since said that if I had kept the company, my earlier health problems would have likely become worse and I might not have survived this long. I expect she is right. I guess I was like the papa robin that wanted to take care of the baby robins. I did that. My family is secure."

Frank shopped for potential buyers, seeking the one he felt would best serve what he had built. He settled on Kane-Miller because, although that company's business interests were varied, the owners had more knowledge of the rendering industry than other interested buyers did. More importantly, he hoped he and his two sons would be able to continue their responsibilities intact after the sale. That plan, of course, worked as long as Kane-Miller owned the company.

The new ownership worked fine for the Franks for 16 years. They all retained their jobs, and they made wise investments with the sale price revenues. Between the sale in 1969 until the middle 1980s, the business continued intact. Frank ran the company without Kane-Miller interference so long as he sent profits to corporate headquarters.

By the early 1980s, however, the successful arrangement was beginning to break down. Kane-Miller was slowly but surely losing interest in manufacturing and moving into other business enterprises. Company owners offered to resell Carolina By-Products to Frank for $19 million, roughly twice what they had paid him for it. He declined, saying the price was too high.

In 1985, Kane-Miller got a better financial deal, but one that in Frank's mind was fiscally unreasonable. Carolina By-Products and three other Kane-Miller companies making up its food ecology group were sold to a freewheeling New York entrepreneur named Ira Heckler for what Frank then and now felt was a staggering price tag of $75 million.

Frank questioned the ridiculously high sale price out of fear that Heckler couldn't sustain the debt and also because he wondered if Heckler cared about maintaining quality instead of profits. Frank worried that the successful business he had built would face collapse or significant reduction. In the ensuing 13 years the company would rotate through five different owners and its presence in Greensboro would be drastically diminished. Frank's fears turned into reality.

"Heckler was strictly a promoter who knew absolutely nothing about the rendering industry," Frank said. "The sale was a bad deal that I opposed but could not prevent. The business was doomed to fail."

Within two years of buying the company, Heckler's high-flying enterprise began to collapse. "All he wanted was money," Frank said. "We made deposits, literally every day, into his account. He didn't care about anything else."

In 1987, Heckler began spinning off and selling chunks of his many businesses, but it wasn't enough. He was in deep debt to Empire Federal Savings Bank in Buffalo, New York, which — because of Heckler's unpaid debts and other bad loans — was also under pressure from the government's Resolution Trust Corporation to clear up financial dealings or face federal sanctions.

By 1988, Heckler had sold 49 percent of Carolina By-Products to the nation's largest rendering company, Darling-Delaware Company of Dallas, Texas, with an option to buy the other 51 percent. But Darling soon ran into its own financial difficulties and subsequently defaulted on a quantity of junk bonds.

"It was the worst financial mess I have ever seen," Frank said of the dealings between Heckler and Darling-Delaware. "The prices were absurd and made no sense. There were a series of minority owners involved, none of whom knew anything about the rendering business."

Among the people connected with the Darling-Delaware ownership was Edward "Rusty" Rose, a Harvard Business School graduate and Dallas businessman. Rose was associated with a group of wealthy individuals known as Texas entrepreneurs, who apparently knew a lot about making money but a lot less about processing animal fats into consumer goods. Rose had the dubious nickname of "The Mortician" among his friends and critics because he reportedly made in excess of $70 million short selling overvalued stock in companies that shortly thereafter withered on the corporate vine. In addition to Rose, investors in Darling-Delaware were Texas millionaires who would later become business partners with George W. Bush, the future president, when he was a part owner of the Texas Rangers major league baseball team.

The new corporate structure brought David Evans in as the new president. His family had once owned Cape Fear Feed Products, the Fayetteville rendering plant that Frank had bought in 1970 for Kane-Miller. That was the beginning of the end for the Franks and other top executives at the company. In a matter of months early in 1988, Frank, his two sons, company president Len Anderson and several other Carolina By-Products officers all left. Their leaving was in frustration as well as regret in watching what they had helped build begin to collapse.

Financial problems and new owners continued during the 1990s; the place was like a revolving door. NationsBank of Charlotte had been a participant in some of the loans involving Heckler and Darling-Delaware, and was increasingly agitated with the results.

"The bank was obviously concerned that it was involved with a company that was half owned by a group in default on bonds and half owned by another group in trouble with the government," said Carolina By-Products' David Rosenstein. "The bank said 'Get another owner or get another banker.'"

In 1991, a group of venture capitalists operating under the title of Capital Resources of Boston and Chemical Ventures Partners of New York bought the company. Five years later, in 1996, a second venture capitalist group under the name of FdeG Associates of New York purchased the company.

Among the FdeG owners were the Fisher brothers, real estate developers; Charles DeGunzburg, a private investor (thus the name FdeG); and the Bronfman family, owners of Seagram liquors. Those owners began attempts to expand their market share and quickly ran into a legal quagmire.

FdeG filed legal action against another rendering company, Valley Proteins of Winchester, Virginia, claiming Valley Proteins' owners had been unfairly diverting suppliers of raw materials to their own company. Valley Proteins, in turn, filed a counter suit alleging it had attempted to buy Carolina By-Products in the early 1990s from Darling-Delaware and had been misled in the negotiations.

The legal debate lingered for several years and cost the two companies between $6 million and $10 million in lost business and legal fees. "In retrospect, it was a bad decision," Rosenstein said of the court battle. "Each was trying to outbid the other. What the two needed was to come together in order to survive and stop beating each other up."

That eventually happened. In August 1998, Valley Proteins, just a few years earlier one of the principals in the on-going legal battle with FdeG, bought Carolina By-Products from FdeG.

Ironically, Valley Proteins shared many similarities with the original Carolina By-Products. One man started Valley Proteins small and grew it successfully, just as Frank had done with Carolina By-Products. Valley Proteins is a private company with interests only in rendering, just as Carolina By-Products. Valley Proteins is owned by Gerald Smith and his two sons, just as Carolina By-Products was under the Frank ownership. The Smiths operate 13 rendering plants in seven states.

Carolina By-Products, however, at the beginning of 2001 was but a shell of what it once was in terms of a visible presence in Greensboro. Production had been greatly curtailed in recent years. No animal by-product processing remains at the local facility. The only manufacturing aspect left at the Randolph Avenue plant site is recycling of restaurant grease services.

The company administration has been relocated to Winchester, Virginia, an hour west of Washington, D.C., where Valley Proteins is headquartered. The company's community interest shown by Frank when he owned it is clearly missing. He was the company cornerstone with the community. While his personal Greensboro involvement is still pronounced, the company's ties to the town are gone.

While Frank said he has no regrets with selling his company under the circumstances at the time, he clearly had pangs of remorse over subsequent events.

"I have not liked to see the company struggle as it has since my sons and I left," he said. "I know I'm biased, but I think we had one of the best companies in the country in our industry. We had contented employees and I was one of them. We had satisfied customers. I don't see much of that now. The administration here is gone. It hurts me to see what has happened. It's a little like losing a child. I was hurt and so were my boys in the way we were treated at the end of our time there. Bill was especially hurt the way he was mistreated. My family has no hardships, but it is difficult for us to witness what has happened to the company and its involvement with the community."

Clearly, Frank's legacy within his former company has been diminished. But his legacy as a respected member of the Greensboro community remains intact even as new generations take over.

It is the Frank family legacy, rather than his former company's, that will continue to thrive and serve the local community. He has ensured that by careful estate planning and creation of a private endowment for the benefit of local people and charities through his family foundation. That will be his continuing contribution to this community well into the future.

Stanley Frank, with sons Bill (left) and Barry, after receving an award from the National Renderers Association, November 11, 1980.

12

Foundation for the Future

When Stanley Frank looks beyond the window in his downtown Greensboro office, he sees far more than the partial skyline of a city in transition. He sees the future, which he believes will be bright. It is also a future he is helping to build.

"In all my travels across this country and in foreign lands, I have never found a community anywhere that I think is superior to Greensboro," Frank said of the city that had been his home for 65 of his 86 years when the calendar year 2001 rolled into reality.

Those aren't Chamber of Commerce words either. They're from the heart of a man who arrived in town on a frosty January morning in 1936 with his entire worldly possessions in one small bag, the clothes on his back, and a $15 a week job driving a meat market and packing house by-product delivery truck.

"I was just looking for a steady job at the time," Frank said of the day he stepped off the train as a total stranger in this southern city that, like other towns across the country, was shaking off the effects of the Great Depression.

Economic conditions at the time were dismal. Gasoline prices bottomed out at 10 cents a gallon, but a large percentage of the populace was not buying because they had no cars or money for fuel. Not long before Frank came to town, then North Carolina Gov. J.C.B. Ehringhaus had moved to help save local communities and stabilize the state's precarious financial situation with drastic measures. In his first year in office, the governor boldly took state control of poverty-possessed public schools from the counties, lowered salaries of teachers and state employees and persuaded the legislature to enact a three-percent sales tax to help the state pay its bills. Few North Carolina governors have been so bold.

Given those sets of circumstances, Frank's anxiety about the future was understandable. "I did not know a single person in the town when I arrived and had no idea how things would work out, what might happen or where I would go."

Well, things worked out just fine, against heavy odds, and Frank didn't go anywhere. Instead, he became a relatively quiet yet significant link to the community's progress and growth. He transformed an out-of-the-mainstream, animal fat rendering plant into an enviable success and established himself as a person who could not only get things done for his adopted community, but get them done efficiently and effectively.

For more than half a century he has given generously of his time and talents to his adopted community. His civic work and philanthropy, however, have never become as recognized as some others because his name was not as well known and he has never craved public attention.

For much of the last half of the 20th century, Stanley Frank has been among those who provided the leadership fuel that helped fire the engines for much of the economic advancement in Greensboro and the surrounding counties. He has steadfastly helped prime the pump for much of the region's progress, particularly in two areas: airline passenger and freight service, and higher education. A primary future goal is to help provide affordable housing for people in need but lacking adequate resources.

A 1980 survey by the business news staff of the *Greensboro Daily News* listed Frank as the third most influential person in the city. If longevity and continuous service had been the primary criteria for that survey, he would easily have ranked number one.

"Stanley Frank has certainly been one of the city's best and longest sustaining corporate cheerleaders," said former Greensboro Mayor Jim Melvin, a Frank watcher over several decades. "He has stayed focused on the business of the community and what needed to be done."

"He has lived and breathed this community," said retired corporate executive Al Schiff of his friend Frank. "If something positive is going on, he has wanted to be a part of it. He wants to remain involved. He's just not a very good baton handler because he doesn't like to hand anything off, to give anything up. His determination for good and the ability to keep going are at the core of his character."

Frank modestly accepts the praise for his community involvement, but isn't fully satisfied with what he, the city and region have been able to achieve during his years of civic service. "I wish," he said, "that I could have done more and the city could have progressed more. I wish I could have given more time for community service." Even so, he has likely given as many hours to community and civic work as anyone else — and more than most — because he has been so dedicated for so long. While many people give a half dozen years to such endeavors, Frank has given a full half-century.

He is what could be described as Greensboro's real-life example of the television commercial mechanical bunny. He has kept on going and going.

And a version of his kind of service will continue far into the future, well after Frank's life is over. He and his wife have created a philanthropic foundation to receive their financial resources, after their deaths, for charitable use so that their wishes for community service will continue.

The Stanley and Dorothy Frank Family Foundation, comprised solely of the couple's assets, was established to make sure that Frank's charitable giving on projects of his preference would continue long beyond his life.

After literally years of careful planning on Frank's part to ensure its viability and credibility, the Frank Foundation was created in late 1997, and funded with approximately $2 million in early 1998. Charitable contributions benefiting the region have been made out of the funds since that date. Significant increased principal funding for the foundation will come following the deaths of Frank, his wife Dorothy, and their two sons, Bill and Barry.

"We want to see our community and state benefit from the things we have been able to accomplish,"

Frank explained. "We want to see people with entrepreneurial spirit get assistance to do good works and to see our educational system get support. We can do that through the family foundation, to ensure that our goals and our wishes continue to make lives better for more people. Our foundation fits those objectives."

Once larger assets exist in the family foundation after the deaths of the Franks, one new focus of the foundation will be to help provide improved housing for more low-income families. "That's one of my major desires," Frank said of his future philanthropy. "I would hope foundation officials, after we are gone, move that goal high on their agenda. It's a worthy and needed objective.

"While I hope the foundation can do whatever it can to assist the most people, I sincerely hope to be able to help finance private residences for people who otherwise couldn't afford their own homes," Frank said. "If people own their homes they will put down roots, will more likely participate actively in the community, and will contribute more to it. I want to see people who have never had the opportunity to own a home get some assistance. Our foundation is a great vehicle to achieve this goal and I hope it is a model for others to accept."

The Frank Family Foundation functions as an arm of the Community Foundation of Greater Greensboro, which will have eventual control of distributions following the deaths of immediate Frank family members.

"The greatest concern for the future of our giving is because of our family situation," Frank said. "We have no grandchildren, no one to carry on the family name, and at some point our family will all be gone," he added with a tinge of regret. "Nobody will be left in our immediate family. Consequently we want to be assured of continuing charities in which we have a particular interest. A constructive way of doing that is through the Community Foundation."

"Because of the family situation, the concept is that the Community Foundation is the most logical source of his ongoing goodwill for Greater Greensboro," said Frank's long-time accountant and legal adviser Carole Bruce. "There will be people [at the Community Foundation] working for the best interest of the city 100 years from now. Stanley explored lots of possibilities and he wanted the foundation to be basically forever, a mechanism for perpetuating his giving after the deaths of his family members. He wanted some sort of continuing entity. This arrangement gives the family foundation a structure forever on the belief that the Community Foundation is more likely to last. This makes good sense for situations like his, where there is not a clear path for a long term future of the family assets once the biological family is all gone."

In addition to the anticipated longevity of the Community Foundation to distribute Frank funds to charities, there are other practical and financial advantages to having the Frank Family Foundation under the larger community foundation umbrella. For example, the Community Foundation was established as a public charity rather than a private foundation, meaning there are no taxes due on investments and no minimum required distributions.

The Frank Family Foundation follows those same public charity federal laws; thus, no taxes are due and no specific requirement exists for contributions. This means that Frank funds can all be used for charities instead of some going for taxes, and distributions can be determined by the family, or later the Community Foundation, without government regulation.

When Frank and his wife created their Family Foundation, it was the only one of its kind under the umbrella of the Community Foundation. That was still the case in 2001. But Frank and Community Foundation officials hope it won't be the last. He hopes other families in similar circumstances will follow his lead.

"We want to work to promote the philosophy of his giving," said Community Foundation President Walker Sanders. "We hope to get more people involved in this approach, to do what the Franks have done."

Sanders' predecessor Worth Durgin, who was instrumental in getting the Frank Foundation established, echoed those sentiments. "We and he wanted to create an example for others to follow, to set a precedent for how others could do the same thing," Durgin said. "It was an opportunity for the Community Foundation to begin the process. His was a prototype. His family situation, with no immediate biological survivors beyond his two sons, was such that he wanted a structure to carry out his intentions for giving. This was the best way for him and his family and was leading the way for others to follow for the good of the community. This structure fit his situation and could fit others."

Organizations similar to the Community Foundation of Greater Greensboro were started in other parts of the country as far back as 1914, the first in Cleveland, Ohio. The Reynolds family of Winston-Salem founded the first in North Carolina in 1919. The independent Greensboro foundation was formed in 1983 — with Frank's assistance — as an umbrella agency to oversee a series of individual private trusts to benefit local community projects and charities.

At the beginning of the 21st century, the Foundation of Greater Greensboro managed approximately $65 million in assets.

Even though the Frank Family Foundation is considered an arm of the Community Foundation, the family foundation directors manage the foundation's investments and determine distributions to charities. That procedure will continue through the lives of Frank, his wife and their two sons. The Community Foundation charges an annual fee for handling ancillary services connected with investments and distributions.

Following the deaths of Frank, his wife and their two sons, the Community Foundation will assume control of the entire estate of Frank and his wife, but the Frank Family Foundation will continue to exist with its mission intact. The Community Foundation will elect its directors, who will serve under the direction of the Franks' stated foundation guidelines.

Frank said he wanted his assets to remain within his family foundation in order to ensure that charities and programs that he has supported during his life will continue to receive benefits after his death. The sons will independently determine if any or how much of their personal assets also go to the Family Foundation at their deaths.

Among the beneficiaries of Frank family assets in the future, in addition to a new emphasis on housing needs, will be institutions of higher education and community programs and services that Frank and his wife have supported generously during several decades of philanthropy. But there will also be additional beneficiaries, just as in the recent past. The airplane cockpit in the two-year-old downtown Children's Museum, for example, is there because of Frank's own financial commitment and his past personal association with a local airplane maintenance company, which he helped recruit for the city, that made the cockpit available.

Frank's assets have grown steadily through the years, mostly because of the success of his rendering business that he purchased in 1953 and through wise investments that Frank has carefully monitored since the sale of his company in 1969. But the size of the Frank estate has also grown because, while Frank and his wife have lived comfortably, they have not lived lavishly — even with abundant resources. The couple has saved money when they could, adding to the value of their estate to be used for community endeavors.

In the early days of their marriage while family resources were few, when Dorothy Frank went shopping, she would often walk to downtown Greensboro from their home a dozen blocks away in Fisher Park in order to save bus fare (four tokens for a quarter). Fifty years later, she still grocery shopped on Tuesdays when senior citizens received five-percent discount. Frank routinely asks for senior citizen discounts in restaurants, even if he is buying hamburgers. Dorothy Frank hangs sheets and towels on an outside clothesline on sunny days because she says she likes the smell of air-dried linens, saving the mechanical clothes drier and high electrical bills for winter months.

"We've been pretty frugal throughout our marriage," Frank acknowledged. "It's the way we were brought up. I learned from my mother the importance of pinching pennies and the importance of productive work without needless spending. Dorothy and I were both raised in family circumstances with not a lot of extra cash. I learned early on that work was necessary and that wasteful spending was not wise. I sometimes still marvel that my family has been so successful. Dorothy and I often talk about how we were able to do it. She reminds me that we've never felt the need to spend an excessive amount of money on ourselves."

Frank's frugality, however, doesn't mean he avoids all luxuries. He is a member of two country clubs, more for easy access to good meals and golf courses, than prestige. The Franks have also made several pleasure trips to Europe, sailing over on the *Queen Elizabeth II* and returning on the Concorde. Such expenses, however, are the exception rather than the rule.

The couple made a nostalgic trip in July 2000, for pleasure and history, to the native land of their parents and grandparents, visiting old family burial plots and other sites in Germany where their ancestors lived in the 1800s.

The one luxury on that trip was flying business class (the equivalent of first class) because of the long hours on the plane. "I told Dorothy that was an expensive way to go and that we could have sailed for a week on the QE II for the cost of the airline tickets." Frank said with a smile, "and she said, 'Fine, let's do that, too.'" He, however, has no plans to book the ship for a return trip across the ocean.

While conceding he enjoyed the trip to Germany to visit ancestral homes in some respects, Frank would just have as soon stayed home. "I owed it to Dorothy to see her father's homeland and to myself to see my mother's home place where our ancestors are buried. But except for that, I'd just as soon stayed right here in this office. I've done a lot of travelling for pleasure as well as business in my lifetime. I prefer staying home now.

"We have lived very well, but our demands are not great. We don't lack for anything we need," Frank said. "We could have spent a lot more money on things that we really didn't need. We've got a beautiful home here, and Dorothy and I each have good cars. We don't need any more of either. I don't want or need to go to the coast or the mountains to a second home. That's an inconvenience, not a wise use of money. I always felt that buying things just because resources were available or because other people had them would be wasting money. I'd rather leave my money for the benefit of charities and this community where the needs are greater. Our money can be of greater use in the community after we're gone."

Dorothy Frank shares her husband's views on charitable giving.

•

Since leaving his former company in 1988, Frank has maintained a small downtown office where he handles investments, stays involved in worthwhile community efforts and dispenses unlimited advice and counsel to steady streams of visitors and callers. His office walls are papered with displays of awards for community projects and philanthropy, both in Greensboro and elsewhere, as is an office trophy case.

Into his 87th year in the summer of 2001, Frank was still an active participant in a series of community projects and civic and charitable endeavors. Those ranged from chairing the nursing school board at UNCG to assignments on committees at the Wake Forest School of Medicine and selection of recipients for the Leadership North Carolina and Leadership Greensboro programs.

Gradually, and more than a little reluctantly, he has begun backing away from past leadership roles in the chamber of commerce, economic development and airport authority duties. That was more from not being asked than lack of desire to be of service.

"There is a whole new generation out there now and they don't know who I am," he said. "I understand that, although I wish it were not that way. I'd still like to be of assistance any way I could. I still do have a strong desire to remain active."

Those who know Frank well say he is diplomatically understating his feelings about being left out or pushed aside because of his age.

"He believes, correctly, that he could still make contributions if people would just ask," his lawyer and adviser Carole Bruce said. " I think he has some really deep hurts over not being asked and I hate that for him."

While Frank may have been asked less often to take on community projects into his middle 80s, he was no less interested in or attuned to those he was still connected with. One, of course, was the administration of his family foundation. His meticulousness was no less pronounced in that effort than it was in his business decades earlier.

"I learned early on that everything had to be perfect and there could not be one penny error in his records," said Bruce, his accountant for more than 30 years and lawyer for two decades. One anecdote illustrates her point.

In the fall of 2000, Frank phoned Bruce with a concern over some financial records of the family foundation involving the quarterly fee from the Community Foundation. The Family Foundation at the time had assets in excess of $2 million.

"Carole," Frank said in that phone call, "I've been looking at the records and the figures are $1.51 off. I know that's not much, but that's just not the way records ought to be kept."

"That's typical of the way he functions," Bruce said. "The small mistake in the figures was not how he felt it was supposed to be done. Most people would never have noticed that error. It was the average of three months fees with balances in four different accounts. And he caught $1.51. That's how meticulous he is."

Bruce was Frank's closest business and legal confidant at the beginning of the 21st century. She began as his accountant in the late 1960s, and became his personal and corporate lawyer in the early 1980s. Bruce and Frank talk every day, many days several times. Their mutual respect and warm feelings toward each other are obvious in their conversations and business relationship.

"I could not have achieved the things I have if it had not been for Carole's solid and continuing advice," Frank said of his association with his lawyer friend. "She had been of great assistance. Sometimes I think that God must have looked down on me and given me Carole. She deserves a lot of credit for my accomplishments."

"I am most respectful of both Stanley and Dorothy," Bruce said. "They do the right thing in almost every situation. They're always very open to listening and talking through things. We have a wonderful relationship, but it's business rather than social. It helps, of course, to have an accountant's mentality in working with him. To some people that kind of thing would be drudgery. But it's fine with me to listen. He likes to get to the core of things. That's one reason we get along so well."

Frank began discussion of his family foundation a decade before it was actually formed. "He began thinking longer term of what would happen after he's gone with two sons and no grandchildren," Bruce explained. "He carefully thought out an ultimate plan. That's where the thought of a foundation first began. He explores every single possibility. The foundation seemed like the right vehicle. Once he decided what to do, he decided to go ahead and set up the foundation so he could enjoy its benefits during his own lifetime rather than waiting until after the deaths of his sons."

Frank's charitable gifts are determined in consultation with his wife, although the ultimate decision is his. Many contributions, specifically to Temple Emanuel and to the local or state symphonies, are at her suggestions. She is not slow to give advice and he generally listens to her requests.

Frank also once made most of the financial decisions for his sons, but as they have grown older he has left more choices to them and encouraged each son to act more independently. "At one time, Stanley handled everything for Bill and Barry," Bruce said. "But over time they have taken over more and moved out on their own with investments. He has supported and encouraged that."

Within the Frank family, there has always existed a continuous requisite respect and relationship between father and sons.

Both sons also have a bit of their father's penchant for careful scrutiny of finances. "Barry is just as focused as his father on details and Bill is just as meticulous in record keeping," Bruce said. "It is total discipline. How many people sometimes let their checking account slide? Well, not any of the Franks. They reconcile things immediately. They are all alike in that regard."

Although Frank's benevolence isn't as well known or as widespread as some other Greensboro families, such as the Bryans and Cones, it has been there over four decades and has made significant positive differences in the lives of many people. The list is long and the pattern of giving consistent, albeit often anonymous.

Bruce is among those who feel Frank has been shortchanged in receiving credit for his community work, in time and dollars. "Stanley and Dorothy have always been extremely generous in their community service and charitable giving," Bruce said. "They have given to a wide variety of charities, not big naming gifts but many smaller ones annually. I don't think Stanley has ever received his due as a contributor to this community. Even so, he doesn't feel he has had a broad philanthropic effect in terms of total dollars or big contributions. But as a person, he was willing to work for the city and get positive things done. I don't think he has been given his just respect for that."

Frank is philosophical about it all.

"When I came to Greensboro, I never thought I would succeed the way I have," he said. "I came to this town as really just a boy with nothing. Over the years I have been able to develop and grow with the community. This area has been very good to me. I had an opportunity to learn the business I was in and then to buy the company. I've had a lot of opportunities to learn and I've tried to take advantage of those chances to improve myself. I have been a very fortunate person. Business, friends, family – these parts of my life have all fallen in place.

"I never had an opportunity for a college degree, but I've always tried to associate myself with people who had more education than I had, so I could learn from them. I've learned a lot from people at Wake Forest University and Guilford College. I learned an enormous amount about finances and business from being associated with the board at First Union National Bank.

"I believe I could have succeeded at whatever I wanted to do because I was determined to succeed, to work hard to achieve. I guess I had confidence in myself. You don't have to be the brightest guy in the world to succeed, but you do have to have the desire and ambition.

"Family is important. If I have any personal regrets about my life it is that I was away so much working and not at home with the children more. I wish I had spent more time with the family. I know the importance of family because I didn't have that stability growing up. But I think I am stronger and probably have a better work ethic because of that. It is a cop-out to say people can't succeed because of a broken home or family situation. That is an excuse, not a reason. Because my father was gone from our home, I knew I had to work harder to find a job and help my mother out of necessity. If my father had been there, I doubt I would have worked so hard so early. Maybe I wouldn't have had such an urge to succeed. I may be better off because of my family situation when I was growing up.

"I've been fortunate in so many ways, and I'm grateful. I'd like to keep doing what I can. But when I can't and my family is gone, I want my assets to keep on working for this community. That will make my life worthwhile well into the future, a kind of payment forward. I want to give back, to help others achieve."

There is no doubt in the minds of Frank's associates that he is fiercely determined to see his foundation succeed well into the future.

His capacity to grow with the community and his ability to lead, albeit mostly behind the headlines, is pronounced if not widely known. His strong determination as well as his strong sense of fairness and understanding have all helped make him a cornerstone of Greensboro's and the region's civic and economic successes over the last half of the 20th century.

Those who know him best say their respect for him grows with time.

He has used his financial resources, his savvy business acumen and his incredibly high energy level for projects to help make life better for those his benevolence has touched. His strong determination as well as his strong sense of fairness and understanding has left an indelible mark for good on his community.

His is a legacy to be admired. And it is one to be emulated.

A Record of Achievement

Stanley Frank's list of civic accomplishments and honors is varied and long, stretching over four decades as he worked to improve the lives of people and organizations across Piedmont North Carolina.

Civic Activities and Honors

Piedmont Triad Airport Authority, member, 1962-1991; chairman, 1972-1991; reappointed to authority, 1994-1997

North Carolina Department of Transportation Aeronautics Council, member and secretary

Greensboro Chamber of Commerce, president, 1972

North Carolina Governor's Committee for Employment of the Handicapped, chairman

North Carolina Symphony, Board of Directors and executive committee

Greensboro Symphony, Board of Directors and executive committee

First Union National Bank, corporate director and chairman of Greensboro bank board

Guilford College, trustee and vice chairman

Creator of Frank Family Scholars Fellowship, Guilford College

Frank Family Science Center, named in his honor at Guilford College

Wake Forest University, Board of Visitors

University of North Carolina at Greensboro, Board of Visitors

Honorary Doctorate of Humanities, Wake Forest University, 1981

National Conference of Christian and Jews, Brotherhood Award, 1974

University of North Carolina School of Nursing, Advisory Board chairman

Greensboro Development Corporation, board member and executive committee

Piedmont Triad Development Corporation, director

Greensboro Sports Council, chairman
Humana Hospital, Greensboro, board chairman

Leadership North Carolina, executive committee

Leadership Greensboro, director

Greensboro Chamber of Commerce, distinguished citizen award, 1980

Initial inductee, Greensboro Business Leaders Hall of Fame, 1980

Greensboro Junior Achievement, board chairman

Greater Greensboro Open Golf Tournament, honorary chairman, 1968

"Who Runs Greensboro?" newspaper series, chosen No. 3 among the top 10 citizens, 1980

UNCG baseball stadium, plaque in his honor, 1999

Business Affiliations

Owner and chairman of the board, Carolina By-Products Company, 1953-1969

Chairman, Carolina By-Products Company, 1969-1988

Chairman, Kane-Miller Food Ecology Group

President, National Renderers' Association

Chairman, Fats and Protein Research Foundation

Board member, Kane-Miller Corporation, 1969-85

Wake Forest University

On the recommendation of the Faculty of

Wake Forest College

the Trustees have conferred upon

Stanley Frank

the degree of

Doctor of Humanities

Given at Winston-Salem in the State of North Carolina
May eighteenth, nineteen hundred eighty-one.

James Ralph Scales
President of the University

Edwin G. Wilson
Provost

Leslie Stokes
President of the Board of Trustees

Elizabeth L. Banks
Secretary of the Board of Trustees

THE NATIONAL CONFERENCE OF CHRISTIANS AND JEWS

PRESENTS ITS BROTHERHOOD CITATION TO

Mr. Stanley Frank

For his dedication to the principles and ideals of the Brotherhood of Man under the Fatherhood of God, as exemplified in his daily life, and

For his devotion and service to religious institutions and causes, and

For his humanitarian service as an energetic leader and worker in behalf of various civic, cultural, educational, and welfare organizations which enrich the life of the community, and

For his helpful contribution to better understanding among all people through association with the National Conference of Christians and Jews

Therefore, as a token of the esteem and appreciation of fellow citizens of all creeds and races, this national Brotherhood Citation is presented this day at the Brotherhood Citation Dinner in

Greensboro, North Carolina
October 10, 1974

NATIONAL CO-CHAIRMEN

William F. May *Robert Murphy* *Oscar Shaw*

PRESIDENT   REGIONAL CHAIRMAN   DINNER CHAIRMAN

David Hyatt *David W. Morehead* *Carl M. Reed*

. . . Twice a year at board meetings, I have listened with awe as faculty and administration have struggled, without a whit of self-consciousness, to define that special quality a Wake Forest education should provide for its students. Always this tension — the imperatives of religious faith against the imperatives of scholarship — underlies the dialogue. I hope we never lose it. It sends us out into the world with perhaps a little more guilt than our contemporaries, but guilt is a concomitant of responsibility, and that's all right, too.

Harold T. P. Hayes
Wake Forest College
Class of 1948

RESOLUTION HONORING

Stanley Frank

upon retirement from
The Board of Directors
of

First Union Corporation

Whereas, Stanley Frank is retiring as a member of this Board on February 19, 1985, after more than twenty years of exemplary service; and

Whereas, during his years as a Director of First Union Corporation, he has served on various committees and has applied his wisdom, experience and judgment in helping to resolve numerous matters and has participated in decisions that have come before these committees and this Board; and

Whereas, during his service as a Director, he has distinguished himself as a successful business executive, while contributing to the civic, social and religious life of the City of Greensboro and the State of North Carolina;

Now, Therefore, Be It Resolved, that the Board of Directors of First Union Corporation expresses its deep appreciation to Stanley Frank for his years of distinguished service and influence as an active member of the Board of Directors.

Be It Further Resolved, that a copy of these resolutions be spread upon the official minutes and the proceedings of this Board and a framed copy to be delivered to Mr. Frank.

Board of Education
of the City of New York

Cottenville High School

This Diploma is awarded to

Stanley Frank

who has satisfactorily completed the

General Course of Four Years

and by proficiency in scholarship and by integrity of character
has merited graduation.

June 30, 1931

Gregory   *William O'Shea*

President Board of Education   Superintendent of Schools

Principal

BOARD OF EDUCATION CITY OF NEW YORK

In recognition and appreciation of exemplary charitable giving

The North Carolina Planned Giving Council

hereby confers upon

Dorothy and Stanley Frank

The 1997 Philanthropist of the Year Award

Vincent J. Gallo, President

November 5, 1997

PIEDMONT TRIAD
INTERNATIONAL AIRPORT

In Appreciation

*The Board of Directors of the Piedmont Triad Airport Authority today
recognizes the termination of the eleventh three-year term of*

Stanley Frank

*as a member of this Board. His record of service commencing in 1962,
includes 18 years as Chairman, with three of those years as both Chairman
and Chief Executive Officer. His contributions to the progress of air
transportation in this community have been substantial.*

*Mr. Frank's vision and leadership contributed significantly
to the construction of the outstanding terminal facility in which the
Authority is now quartered. His concept of the Airport as one serving the
Triad community has resulted in the enlargement of the Board to include
representatives from the City of Winston-Salem and Forsyth County.*

*His abilities in financial matters have enabled the Authority to achieve
an excellent reputation for its fiscal policies. His persistence and influence
have assisted in the obtaining of federal grants for the expansion of
runways and taxiways and the installation of safety devices upon the
Airport. His foresight concerning the role of the Airport in economic
growth has resulted in bringing onto the Airport air-related businesses
which have enriched this area and provided jobs for numerous employees.
The list of his accomplishments is almost endless —
certainly too numerous to itemize further in this resolution.*

*Suffice it to say, the excellent position which the Airport
operated by this Authority now occupies is due in good measure to the
efforts of Stanley Frank. He deserves, and we extend to him, the
appreciation not only of this Board, but of the entire Triad area, for his
years of valuable and useful service to this Board and to the
Airport which it owns and operates.*

F. Hudnall Christopher, Chairman
Piedmont Triad International Airport

May 27, 1997
Date

The Presidential Award

Presented in recognition of distinguished service to the
Board of Trustees of the North Carolina Symphony Society, Inc.,
for invaluable leadership in support of the Symphony as

Chairman of the Development Committee to

Stanley Frank

This seventeenth day of November, 1978

Harvey M. Wagner

Harvey M. Wagner
President
North Carolina Symphony Society, Inc.